EYEWITNESS
ANCIENT ROME

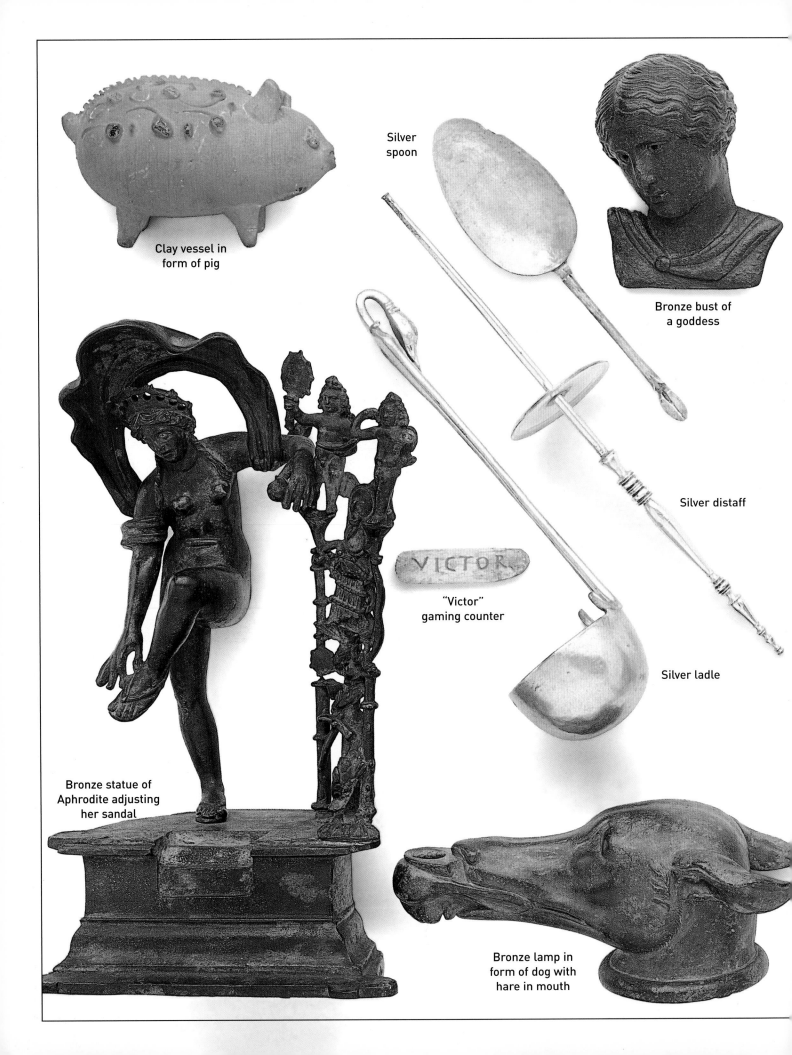

Clay vessel in form of pig

Silver spoon

Bronze bust of a goddess

Silver distaff

"VICTOR"

"Victor" gaming counter

Silver ladle

Bronze statue of Aphrodite adjusting her sandal

Bronze lamp in form of dog with hare in mouth

Ostrogothic brooches

Gold dolphin earrings

EYEWITNESS
ANCIENT ROME

Written by
DR SIMON JAMES

Bronze bust of Minerva

Bronze hero in combat

Gold glass picture of a *retiarius* (a type of gladiator)

In association with
THE BRITISH MUSEUM

Bronze toilet set for the baths

Silver brooch with a bust of Zeus

DK | Penguin Random House

Project editor Susan McKeever
Senior art editor Julia Harris
Managing editor Sophie Mitchell
Special photography Christi Graham and Nick Nicholls of
The British Museum and Karl Shone

RELAUNCH EDITION (DK UK)

Senior editor Chris Hawkes
Senior art editor Spencer Holbrook
US senior editor Margaret Parrish
Jacket editor Claire Gell
Jacket designer Laura Brim
Jacket design development manager Sophia MTT
Producer, pre-production Francesca Wardell
Producer Janis Griffith
Managing editor Linda Esposito
Managing art editor Philip Letsu
Publisher Andrew Macintyre
Publishing director Jonathan Metcalf
Associate publishing director Liz Wheeler
Design director Stuart Jackman

RELAUNCH EDITION (DK INDIA)

Project editor Bharti Bedi
Project art editor Nishesh Batnagar
DTP designer Pawan Kumar
Senior DTP designer Harish Aggarwal
Picture researcher Nishwan Rasool
Jacket designer Dhirendra Singh

First American Edition, 1990
This American Edition, 2015

Published in the United States by DK Publishing
345 Hudson Street, New York, New York 10014
A Penguin Random House Company

15 16 17 18 19 10 9 8 7 6 5 4 3 2 1
001—ED629—Jun/15

Published in Great Britain by Dorling Kindersley Limited.
A catalog record for this book is available from the Library of Congress.

ISBN 978-1-4654-3568-2 (Paperback)
ISBN 978-1-4654-3569-9 (ALB)

DK books are available at special discounts when
purchased in bulk for sales promotions, premiums,
fund-raising, or educational use. For details, contact:
DK Publishing Special Markets, 345 Hudson Street,
New York, New York 10014 or SpecialSales@dk.com.

Printed by South China Printing Co. Ltd., China

A WORLD OF IDEAS:
SEE ALL THERE IS TO KNOW
www.dk.com

Bronze boar being led to sacrifice

Bronze *lar* (household god)

Contents

Clay ointment flask in form of hare

The rise of Rome

According to legend, Rome was founded in 753 BCE by twin brothers Romulus and Remus, sons of the god Mars. Over the next thousand years, it became the capital of one of the most powerful empires in history. Rome began as a small city-state ruled by kings. In 509 BCE, the last king was driven out and Rome became a republic. The early Roman civilization was influenced by two neighbouring peoples – the Etruscans and the Greeks.

The Etruscans

The Etruscan people lived in a group of city-states, north of Rome, and were highly influenced by Greece. They were great traders, architects, and engineers.

Etruscan art
This Etruscan bronze sculpture shows a three-horse chariot running over a fallen man. The Etruscans may have given Rome the idea of chariot racing (p.34).

Greek art
The Romans admired and copied the realistic figures in Greek art.

The Greeks

The Greeks had founded colonies across southern Italy and had built many wealthy cities with fine temples and houses. These Greek colonies eventually came under Roman control, bringing with them their art and culture.

River god
This clay face shows that the Greeks were skilled potters.

Aphrodite
The Romans modelled their goddess Venus on the Greek goddess of love, Aphrodite.

Elephant army

In 218 BCE, a Carthaginian general named Hannibal marched his army and 37 elephants from Hispania (modern-day Spain) to Italy over the Alps. Hannibal won many battles in Italy, but never captured Rome. He fought on for years in Italy, while the Romans attacked Hannibal's bases in Spain and north Africa. Finally, the Carthaginians withdrew. Rome had won new lands, but at a high price.

Victory symbol

The Romans thought of the spirit of military victory as a goddess, as shown in this bronze statuette.

Goddess holds a crown of laurel leaves

Expansion

After the wars with Carthage, Rome defeated other powerful states to the east. The generals who won these conflicts began to compete with each other for power, which led to bitter civil wars.

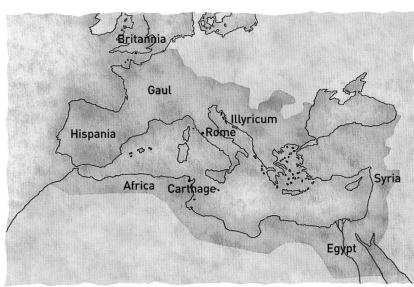

The shadow of Rome

The Roman Empire was divided into provinces. Most of the Mediterranean had fallen to Rome by 50 CE and the Empire was at its height by the 2nd century CE.

Julius Caesar

General Julius Caesar defeated his rivals and began to rule Rome like a king. Eventually he was assassinated by a group of Roman senators (p.16).

A ship of war

The Romans learned from Carthage how to fight at sea. The clay plaque above shows a war-galley, propelled by oars, with a ram at the front that was used to sink other vessels.

The emperors

Rome was not always ruled by emperors. For nearly 500 years, Rome was a republic ruled by an elected group called the Senate. But the Republic collapsed in the chaos of the civil wars both before and after Julius Caesar's death. In 27 BCE, Caesar's adopted son, Octavian (later called Augustus), reformed the state and brought peace back to the Roman world. He became the first emperor of Rome, and when he died in 14 CE, he passed the new throne to his adopted son, Tiberius. Rome was to be ruled by emperors for the next 400 years.

Caligula went mad and was murdered: reigned 37–41 CE

Claudius conquered Britain: reigned 41–54 CE

Nero was the last of Augustus's family: reigned 54–68 CE

Heads and tales
Coins were a good way to display the image of the emperor and his deeds. These are coins of Tiberius's successors.

A Roman triumph
When an emperor won a great victory, he would be granted a parade called a triumph. This gave him the right to lead his soldiers and prisoners through Rome, while the people cheered.

Mad emperor
Some emperors went mad with power. Many Romans blamed Nero for starting the great fire of Rome in 64 CE, so that he could build himself a new capital in its ruins.

Emperor's weapon
This spectacular scabbard depicts Emperor Tiberius. It was found in the River Rhine in Germany.

Tiberius receiving his nephew, the general Germanicus

The colour of power
Purple, the most expensive dye, was largely reserved for the emperor's clothes. Senators wore togas with a purple band.

Purple dye came from murex seashells

Laurel for a crown

Roman emperors did not wear gold crowns because they did not want to be thought of as kings. But they often wore laurel wreaths to symbolize their success and military power – particularly after a conquest.

The jewelled crown was added much later

Cameo of a god

The carved gem above shows the emperor Augustus. He was proclaimed a god when he died.

Julia and Livia

Here Augustus's wife, Livia, is shown as the goddess Juno, and his daughter, Julia, as the helmeted goddess Roma. Livia was married to Augustus for 53 years, and had considerable influence over him.

Drusilla

This stone portrait depicts one of the younger women in Augustus's family, probably Drusilla.

Heir to the throne

Often the emperor adopted a promising young man to succeed him when he died. Emperor Antoninus Pius adopted Lucius Verus, shown here in this fine bronze bust.

Portrait of Emperor Tiberius

Traces of wood from the scabbard are stuck to the steel blade

A legion's eagle standard in a shrine

The legions

The Roman army was a powerful fighting force. It was made up of well-trained, professional foot soldiers called legionaries. Each legion consisted of about 5,000 soldiers, who were organized into smaller fighting units called centuries. In the second century CE, there were 150,000 legionaries in the Roman army. Modern replicas of legionary equipment are shown on these pages.

Crest
Centurions and other officers wore crested helmets, so that their men could see them in battle.

Crest shown in position but not attached

Head protector
This helmet was designed to protect the head, face, and neck without blocking vision or hearing.

Metal jacket
Body armour was made of metal strips held by leather straps on the inside. It was heavy, but flexible, and soldiers had to help each other to put it on.

Rome's Capitoline Hill survived capture by the Gauls in 390 BCE when sacred geese woke up the sleeping soldiers.

Tunic
A coarse woollen tunic was worn under the armour. In later times, Roman soldiers wore short breeches under their tunics.

Belting up
The *balteus*, or belt, was a soldier's badge of office, worn with the tunic at all times. The decorated leather strips gave an extra layer of protection in battle.

The heavy pendants weighed the strips down

Long point of the pilum designed to pierce enemy's shield

Woollen cloak

Leather bottle for water or wine

Pack for personal items and rations for three days

Javelin
The spear (far left) was replaced by the heavy javelin, or *pilum* (left). A shower of these flying through the air would break the enemy's charge.

Marius's mule
Each legionary carried a pack, which held a tool kit and a dish and pan. The pack weighed 40 kg (90 lb) or more, and often had to be carried up to 30 km (20 miles) in a day. Soldiers were called "Marius's mules" after the general who introduced the pack.

Mattock for digging ditches

The sword's grip was made of wood, although bone and ivory were also used

Dagger had a double-edged blade

Turf cutter for building turf ramparts

Boots
Military sandals *(caligae)* were strong and well ventilated, with patterns of iron hobnails specially designed to survive miles of marching.

Sword and dagger
A *pugio*, or dagger, was worn on the left, and a *gladius*, or short sword, on the right. The sword was a terrible stabbing weapon, short enough to wield easily in the crush of battle.

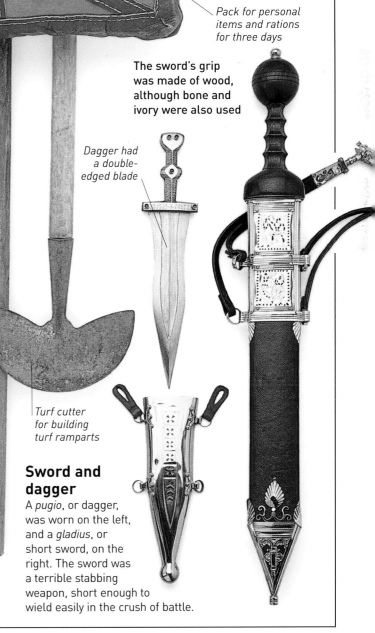

Army life

By the beginning of the 1st century CE, the Romans had conquered most of their empire. Now soldiers were kept busy guarding the borders of the conquered provinces and stamping out rebellions. Many of the wars at this stage were fought to stop outsiders from invading the provinces. Every legion was supported by non-citizen auxiliary soldiers, who were usually recruited from conquered peoples throughout the Empire.

Catapult bolts

Soldiers used catapults to hurl darts and stones at the enemy. These are the iron tips from wooden darts, or "bolts".

A province won

Julius Caesar conquered Gaul in the 50s BCE. This Victorian painting shows the defeated Gallic leader, Vercingetorix, entering the Roman camp to surrender his arms. Caesar is seated on the red platform in the distance.

An auxiliary soldier

Auxiliaries were used to guard and patrol the vast borders of the Roman Empire.

Shield cover

Soldiers' wooden shields had a metal cover over the handle. This could be used to hit the enemy at close range.

A Roman fort

Soldiers spent the winter months in stone or timber forts. Below is the rebuilt gate of a fort in England.

The spoils of war

This ivory plaque shows weapons seized in war. Plunder from conquests helped to pay the troops and finance the splendour of Rome. The conquests also brought several million slaves to Italy.

Scaly protection
Fabric shirts covered with bronze scales were a common type of armour.

The cavalry
The auxiliary cavalry (soldiers who fought on horseback) were highly paid because they had to buy their own horses. Most auxiliary cavalry came from Gaul, Holland, and Thrace (Bulgaria). The cavalry were the eyes of the army, patrolling ahead of the legions, guarding their flanks in battle, and pursuing defeated enemies.

A parade
This carving shows legionaries and galloping cavalrymen. The legionaries sport crests on top of their helmets (p.10).

Harness fitting
This is one of a set of silvered harness fittings from Xanten in Germany.

Cavalry spur
Riders used spurs attached to their shoes to urge their horses on.

Barbarians
This wild entanglement of limbs, horses, and armour is a relief (carving) from a stone coffin. It shows Roman cavalry fighting northern barbarians. The artist gives a fine impression of the chaos of battle.

Spearheads
Auxiliary soldiers used light javelins for throwing (p.11), and heavier spears for thrusting at close range. These iron spearheads come from Dorset in England. The wooden shafts rotted long ago.

Champing at the bit
Roman horse harnesses were similar to those of today. Leather reins and a bridle were linked to a bit which went in the horse's mouth.

Life of a soldier

The army played an important role in Roman society. Many poorer people joined the army because it offered a good standard of living and the chance to learn a skill or trade. Soldiers were rewarded at the end of their military service—retired legionaries were given grants of land or money, and auxiliary soldiers were granted Roman citizenship. Settlements grew up around the army camps, some of which developed into cities, such as York in England. Many soldiers serving in the provinces married local women, which helped to spread Roman culture and traditions across the Empire.

Parade mask
In peacetime, soldiers spent a lot of time training. Cavalrymen often wore elaborate armor for parades. This bronze mask is from a helmet probably made for mock cavalry battles.

Clay plaque
Soldiers made their own materials, like this clay plaque for a roof. It shows the name and emblem of the 20th legion—a charging boar.

Hadrian's Wall
At Emperor Hadrian's command, the army built a great stone wall to protect Britain from the Caledonian tribes of Scotland. Legionaries built the wall and the auxiliaries guarded it. The wall ran for 75 miles (120 km).

A fanciful view of a legionary, complete with shield and spear

Elaborate hairstyle on mask

Tombstone
This broken tombstone belonged to the daughter of a Roman standard bearer stationed in Lancashire, England.

Bronze document
When auxiliaries in the provinces completed 25 years of service, they were usually granted Roman citizenship. To prove their new status, some soldiers had bronze copies of the official document made, like this one from Cheshire in England.

The emperor's image and titles

The lid is on the inside

Purse
Soldiers carried cash in leather or bronze purses like this one on the left. Worn like a bracelet, it could only be opened when it was taken off, so it was hard to rob.

Forgotten hoard
These gold pieces, more than four years' pay for a legionary, were buried in Kent, England, just after the Romans invaded Britain.

Citizens and slaves

Roman society was divided into three main groups of people: Roman citizens, non-citizens (or provincials—people who came from outside Rome), and slaves. Citizens themselves were divided into different ranks. Senators were elected by the people and were usually wealthy nobles. The next rank of citizens were the equestrians, who served in the army and helped to run the government. Roman slaves generally led hard lives, although some were well treated and even powerful.

SPQR
These letters found on inscriptions stand for *Senatus Populusque Romanus* (the Senate and people of Rome).

Brooch
The brooch, or *fibula*, was used for fastening cloaks at the shoulder.

Sprung safety pin was behind decorative front of brooch

Rings
Rings were worn by men and women. Gold rings were a badge of rank for equestrians, and rings with carved stones were used to seal documents.

Gold signet ring

Silver rings showing Hercules (left) and Mars (below)

Ring made of gold coin

Rods were tied together with a strap

Ax

Symbol of power
Important officials were escorted by *lictors*, men who carried the *fasces* (an ax in a bundle of rods). This symbolized their authority to punish people.

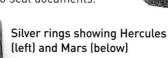

Nobleman

Sacrificial assistant

Priest

Peasant

Men's gear
Roman men wore a knee-length sleeveless tunic with various types of cloak. On formal occasions citizens wore the heavy white toga.

Citizen in toga

Senator

Headed paper
The back of this wooden writing tablet shows the stamp of the procurator of Britain – the official who collected taxes and paid the army in Britain. The procurator was of a lower rank than the governor, a senator who commanded the army and administered justice.

On the other side there was a layer of wax to write on (p.40)

Escape from the arena
Most Roman gladiators were slaves, but success in the arena could win them their freedom. The bone ticket (above) grants freedom to a gladiator called Moderatus.

The forum
Each Roman town had a forum, a market square with public buildings around it. The forum in Rome (above) was the heart of the capital. On the right is the *curia*, or senate house. Nearby were the imperial palace and the Colosseum.

Hair and beards
Roman men were keen followers of fashion. The man shown in this bronze bust sports the thick hair and clipped beard fashionable around 130 CE. Over time, longer beards became more popular.

Clipped beard fashionable around 130 CE

Women in Rome

Roman women were expected to be dignified wives and good mothers. Girls were only educated up to primary standard, if at all. Wealthy women could enjoy a good deal of independence, especially if they were widows. At the other end of the scale, large numbers of women were slaves, ranging from ladies' maids to farm workers.

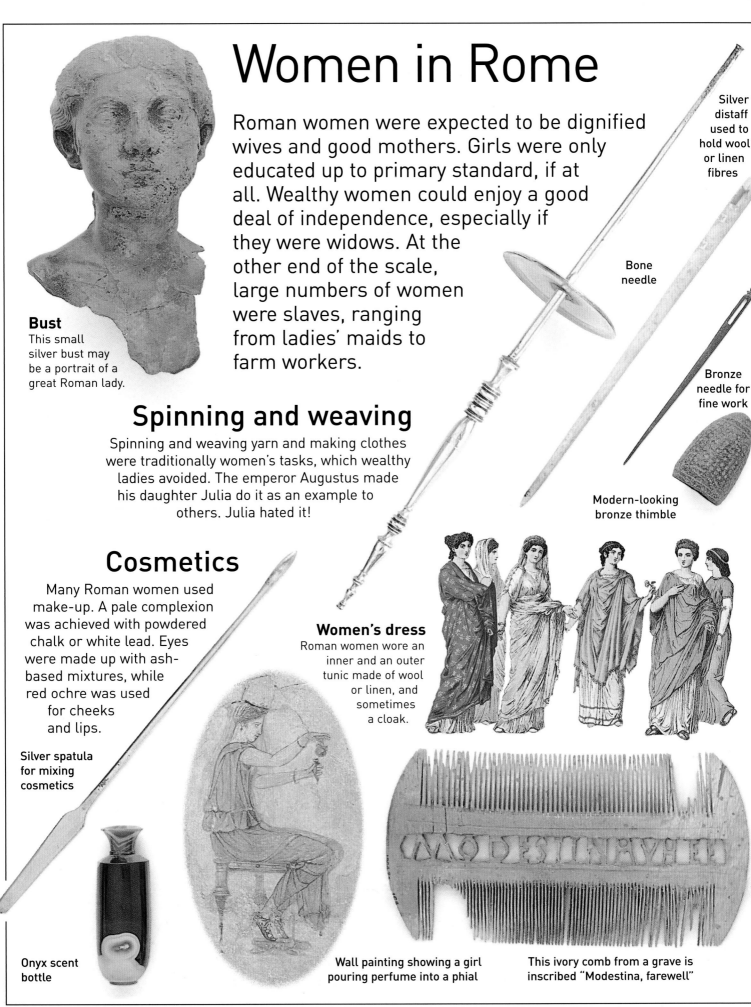

Bust
This small silver bust may be a portrait of a great Roman lady.

Silver distaff used to hold wool or linen fibres

Bone needle

Bronze needle for fine work

Modern-looking bronze thimble

Spinning and weaving

Spinning and weaving yarn and making clothes were traditionally women's tasks, which wealthy ladies avoided. The emperor Augustus made his daughter Julia do it as an example to others. Julia hated it!

Cosmetics

Many Roman women used make-up. A pale complexion was achieved with powdered chalk or white lead. Eyes were made up with ash-based mixtures, while red ochre was used for cheeks and lips.

Silver spatula for mixing cosmetics

Women's dress
Roman women wore an inner and an outer tunic made of wool or linen, and sometimes a cloak.

Onyx scent bottle

Wall painting showing a girl pouring perfume into a phial

This ivory comb from a grave is inscribed "Modestina, farewell"

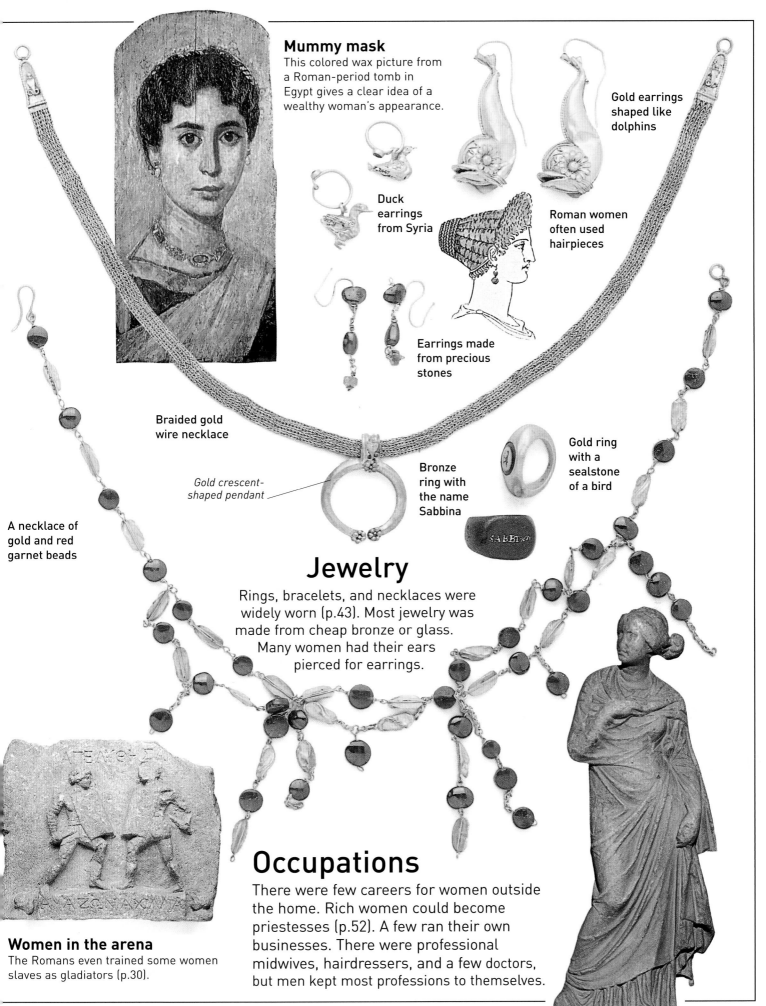

Mummy mask
This colored wax picture from a Roman-period tomb in Egypt gives a clear idea of a wealthy woman's appearance.

Gold earrings shaped like dolphins

Duck earrings from Syria

Roman women often used hairpieces

Earrings made from precious stones

Braided gold wire necklace

Gold crescent-shaped pendant

Bronze ring with the name Sabbina

Gold ring with a sealstone of a bird

SABBINA

A necklace of gold and red garnet beads

Jewelry
Rings, bracelets, and necklaces were widely worn (p.43). Most jewelry was made from cheap bronze or glass. Many women had their ears pierced for earrings.

Occupations
There were few careers for women outside the home. Rich women could become priestesses (p.52). A few ran their own businesses. There were professional midwives, hairdressers, and a few doctors, but men kept most professions to themselves.

Women in the arena
The Romans even trained some women slaves as gladiators (p.30).

Growing up

Family outing
Roman children dressed like their parents, and often went with them to official ceremonies. This detail from an Augustan monument shows members of the emperor's family in a sacrificial procession.

For some lucky Roman children, growing up consisted simply of play and school. Some wealthy parents hired tutors to teach their children at home, but most sent their children to school from the age of seven to eleven to learn the basics of mathematics and grammar. School ran from dawn until noon, and there was much learning by heart. Girls rarely got more than a basic education, after which they had to learn household skills at home. Most children from poorer families received no schooling at all, but were sent out to work from an early age.

Young boy
This marble bust is of a boy at about the age of five. The strange hair curl shows that he worships the god Isis (p.50).

Hair curl

Dozing slave
Many Roman children were slaves. The oil flask (left) depicts a slave boy dozing on a box while he waits for his master to return. Many slaves worked very long hours, so he may be taking a nap while he can.

A boy's life
This marble relief shows the stages in a boy's life, from being nursed by his mother to reciting to his father. The middle scene shows him riding a donkey chariot.

Wear and tear on doll

Toxic toy
This toy camel from Egypt would not be allowed into the shops today – it is made of poisonous lead.

Marbles
Marbles were already popular toys in Roman times, and were made of a variety of materials.

Glass marbles

Pottery marbles

Elaborately plaited hair

Rag doll
This much-loved and rather moth-eaten rag doll from Roman times was well preserved in the dry soil of Egypt.

Young girl
This fine marble portrait shows a girl of about ten. Her hair was originally coloured red, and is styled like that of adult women of the time (about 200 CE). Roman children were brought up to look and behave just like their parents.

Chariot
This model chariot suggests that the thrills of the racetrack were as exciting to Roman children as racing cars are today.

Marriage ceremony

The couple exchange vows and clasp hands to symbolize their union. The groom is holding the marriage contract.

Family life

The idea of the family was very important to the Romans. The father, or *paterfamilias*, held complete power over his entire family. He had, in theory, power of life and death over his children. Wives controlled the running of the house and its finances, and supervised the children until they went to school (p.20). Larger households also had a number of slaves. Many led hard lives, but others were sometimes treated as members of the family.

A Roman wedding

In Roman times, marriages often took place for financial or political reasons. Brides wore a special dress and a bright orange veil. The marriage ceremony was held at the bride's house or at a nearby shrine. A sacrifice was offered to win the approval of the gods.

Engagement rings

The groom often gave his future bride a ring engraved with clasped hands.

Missing face

This portrait shows Emperor Severus with his wife and sons, Caracalla and Geta. After Severus died, Caracalla murdered Geta. His image was later removed from the portrait.

Slaves and pets

Wealthy Roman homes would have seemed crowded to modern eyes, with slaves scurrying around cleaning and carrying. The household would also include working animals, such as guard dogs and cats, to chase rats. Pets were kept mainly for the children.

Freed slave

Ex-slave Hedone set up this plaque to the goddess Feronia, who was popular with freed slaves.

Sad slave?

This model shows a kitchen slave weeping. He is either unhappy with his hard life, or grinding a strong onion!

Dog collar

Guard dog

Many Romans kept fierce guard dogs chained by the door to deter thieves.

Dog tag

This bronze dog tag says: "Hold me if I run away, and return me to my master Viventius on the estate of Callistus."

Household gods

Most Romans were religious and respected their many gods (p.50), especially the gods and spirits who protected the household. Every home had its own shrine at which the family would worship daily. It was also important to remember the family ancestors. Most people would regularly go to the family graves to pay homage to the dead. (p.56).

Crest on snake's head

Dolphin-headed drinking horn

Lar
The *lar* was a spirit of the family's ancestors. This bronze *lar* is pouring wine from a drinking horn in one hand while holding a libation bowl in the other (p.52).

Libation bowl was used to pour liquids onto the sacrificial fire on the altar

Snake spirit
The household also had its own protective spirit, which was depicted as a bearded snake (see the shrine below).

A ball of incense about to be burned on an altar

Genius
This was the personal protective spirit of a man (a woman was guarded by a Juno).

Household shrine
This *lararium*, or household shrine, from a Pompeii house (left) is shaped like a little temple.

Dedicated ex-slaves
Romans often had very good relations with their slaves, and when they freed them, they often became their patrons. This tomb monument shows Lucius Antistius Sarculo and his wife Antistia. The inscription records that the monument was set up by Rufus and Anthus, two of their freed slaves. Clearly Rufus and Anthus greatly admired their former masters. The ex-slaves must have become wealthy themselves to be able to afford such a splendid monument.

House and home

Wealthy Roman homes were usually of the same basic design. The front door opened into an atrium or hall, which had an opening to the sky and a pool in the floor to catch rainwater. A colonnaded garden at the back added to the airy feeling of the house. Although the walls were brightly painted and the floors richly decorated with mosaics, there was surprisingly little furniture. Only the wealthy lived in luxury. Most people lived in rural poverty, or in tall, crowded city apartments above rows of shops. The blocks of flats had no running water, and fire was a constant risk.

Wildlife
As in Italy today, houses and gardens had their own brand of wildlife: scorpions in dark corners, and lizards basking on sunny walls.

Cat among the pigeons
This mosaic shows a cat which has just caught a pigeon. The picture is made up of thousands of tiny pieces of coloured stone, each about 5 mm (0.2 in) square.

Lizards like this bronze model still live in the ruins of Pompeii

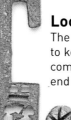

Lock and key
The Romans used locks to keep out burglars. The complicated shape of the end of the key (below) fitted through a keyhole into the pattern of holes in the hidden bolt (left).

Pattern of holes in bolt matches key shape

Lock with special shape on end

Cogs connected to handles on the outside

A strong box
This strongbox has two sliding bolts in the lid (shown turned over). These were operated by turning the cogs from the outside. Boxes such as this would have been used to store money and valuables.

Couch end
This carved ivory plaque from the side of a couch shows Cupid, the god of love, hovering above Bacchus, the god of wine, clutching a bunch of grapes.

Elephant leg

This brightly coloured bronze elephant's head was in fact a leg from a piece of furniture – probably a couch. It may have been modelled on one of the many elephants brought over from Africa to fight in the arena (p.32).

The foot looks like a lion's paw

Lighting up time

Romans lit their houses with oil lamps of pottery or bronze. The lamps burned olive oil, which was quite expensive and not very bright. It was often a better idea to go to bed as soon as it got dark!

The ears make brackets for attaching the leg

Oil was poured into this hole, which was originally covered with a hinged lid

An atrium

Wealthy Romans received guests in the atrium. This drawing of a Pompeii house shows the central pool and the skylight.

Position of couch end

Mule-headed

This bronze couch end is decorated with a satyr (woodland god) and a mule's head. The position of the couch end can be seen in the reconstruction above.

Copper and silver inlay

Part of a wall painting from Stabiae, near Pompeii

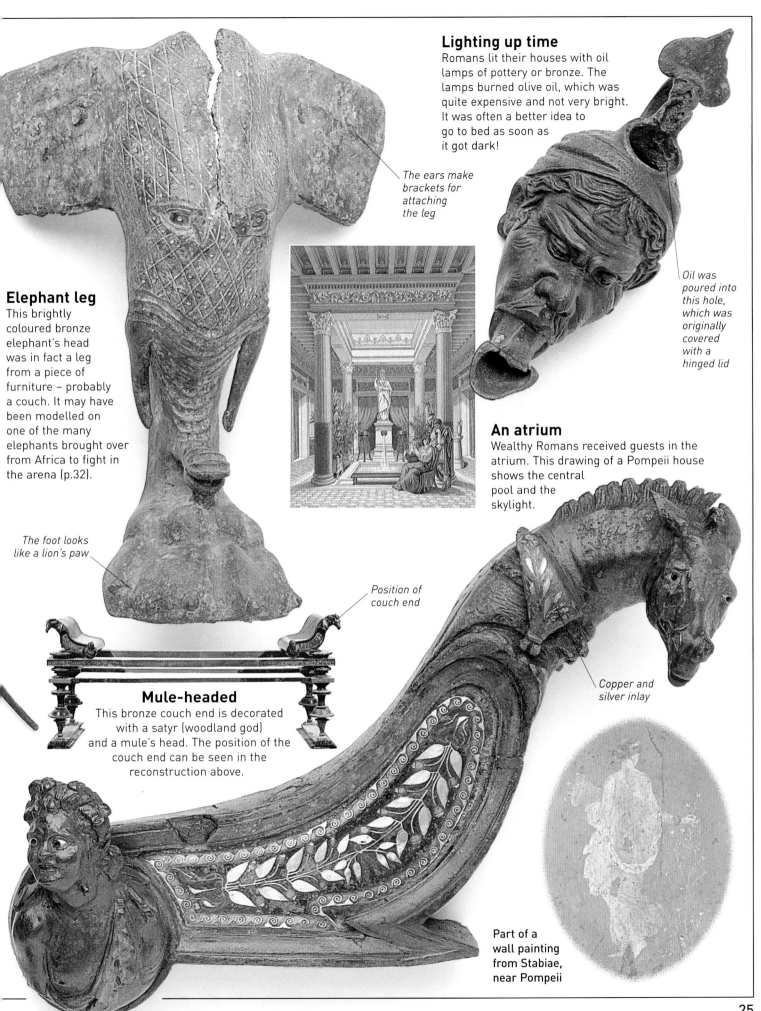

Master builders

The Romans were skilled builders, constructing temples, country houses, and magnificent public buildings from stone, brick, and marble. They made great use of arches, and even invented the dome. The Romans also had sound engineering skills—they built aqueducts to deliver water supplies to cities and constructed roads and bridges that are still in use today.

Pont du Gard, France
This three-story stone bridge carried an aqueduct that ran for about 30 miles (50 km). The water flowed through a covered channel along the top.

Plumb bob
A piece of string attached to a simple bronze weight gave a perfectly vertical line to make sure walls were straight.

Foot-rule is divided into 12 Roman inches

Bronze rule
This folding rule was easily carried on a belt or in a bag. It is one Roman foot long (11⅝ in [296 mm]).

Dividers are tightened with a wedge

Dividers
Engineers used dividers like these when working with scale plans and models. The gap between the lower points is always twice that between the upper points.

Bronze square
Used for checking right-angles, this tool would have been useful to masons, carpenters, and mosaic makers.

A Roman road
Roads were usually very straight. They were built with a camber (hump) so that rainwater drained into ditches. Roads were made up of several levels and were covered with gravel or stone slabs.

Chisel
Romans used chisels like this iron one when they worked with wood. These tools were especially useful for making roof frames.

Roman plumbing

Water supplies were very advanced in many Roman cities. The great aqueducts supplied a number of water outlets, especially public fountains (from which most people fetched their household water in buckets). Bathhouses had their own supplies, as did public toilets. Larger private houses often had running water, while also collecting rainwater from the roof (see the atrium on p.25). Elaborate systems of lead pipes fed the water to these buildings, and a system of underground sewers carried away the waste.

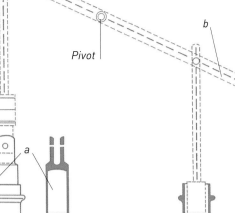

Working pump

This reconstruction of a water pump shows how it worked. Two simple pumps were joined together. Each half had a piston (a) which, when raised by the handle (b), sucked water into the cylinder (c) through a one-way valve (d). When the piston was pushed down, the water was forced into the outlet pipe (e) and out through another valve (f). The two cylinders acting in turn sent a jet of water out of the central pipe (g).

Pivot

water level

Pompeii fountain

Fountains worked by gravity. The statue depicts a boy holding a goose, and the weight of the water in a hidden tank forced the jet out of the goose's mouth.

Multi-seat toilet

A water channel under the seats carried away sewage.

Valve

Preserved pump

Pumps like this well-preserved lead one were used to raise water to a higher level. The writer Vitruvius records that they were used to fill the tanks of public fountains, like the one above left.

The valve cover allowed water to flow out, but shut when it tried to go the other way

This section has been cut away to reveal the outlet valves and to show the pipe joints

The Colosseum

The Colosseum in Rome is a marvel of engineering. Opened by Emperor Titus in 80 CE, it provided seating for 50,000 spectators. The arched vaults on the ground floor formed 80 entrances, so that visitors could enter and leave quickly. A huge canvas awning could be stretched over the top to provide shade from the sun, and a massive iron chandelier lit up the arena at night. The Romans flocked to the Colosseum to watch trained fighters called gladiators fight to the death. These games were paid for by the emperors and other important Romans who wanted to win popularity with the people.

The weight of the seating was carried on arches

The seats nearest the front were reserved for the wealthy

The maze of corridors, cells, and machinery beneath the arena

Blood and sand
The arena was covered in sand to soak up any spilled blood. Beneath it was a maze of cells and passages. When it was time to fight, the men and animals were brought up in elevators and released through trapdoors.

Sea battle
It was once thought that gladiators fought "sea battles" on water in the arena. The event is imagined here by an 18th-century artist, but is no longer believed to be true.

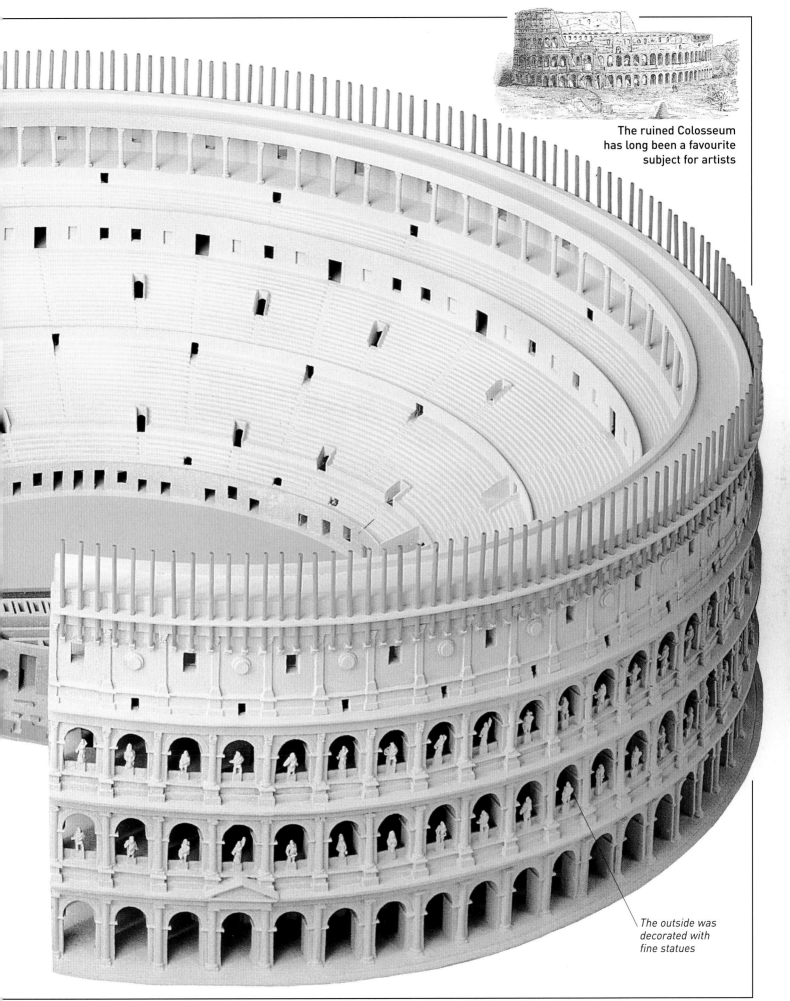

The ruined Colosseum
has long been a favourite
subject for artists

*The outside was
decorated with
fine statues*

29

Mortal combat

Most gladiators were either slaves or criminals who had been trained to fight in special schools. There were various types of gladiators, each with distinct weapons and costumes. If they were lucky, they survived to win their freedom. Many Romans thought the gladiator's way of life was glamorous. Some men even volunteered to be gladiators, and the emperor Commodus shocked Rome by fighting in the arena himself. For many of these trained murderers, however, life was brutal and short.

Bronze shield
A small bronze shield like this might have been carried by a Thracian (p.33). It did not offer much protection in a fight.

The net man

This glass picture shows a type of gladiator called a *retiarius* (net man). He carried a weighted net to catch his opponent, and a trident to stab him. If he lost his net, the unarmoured *retiarius* was usually doomed.

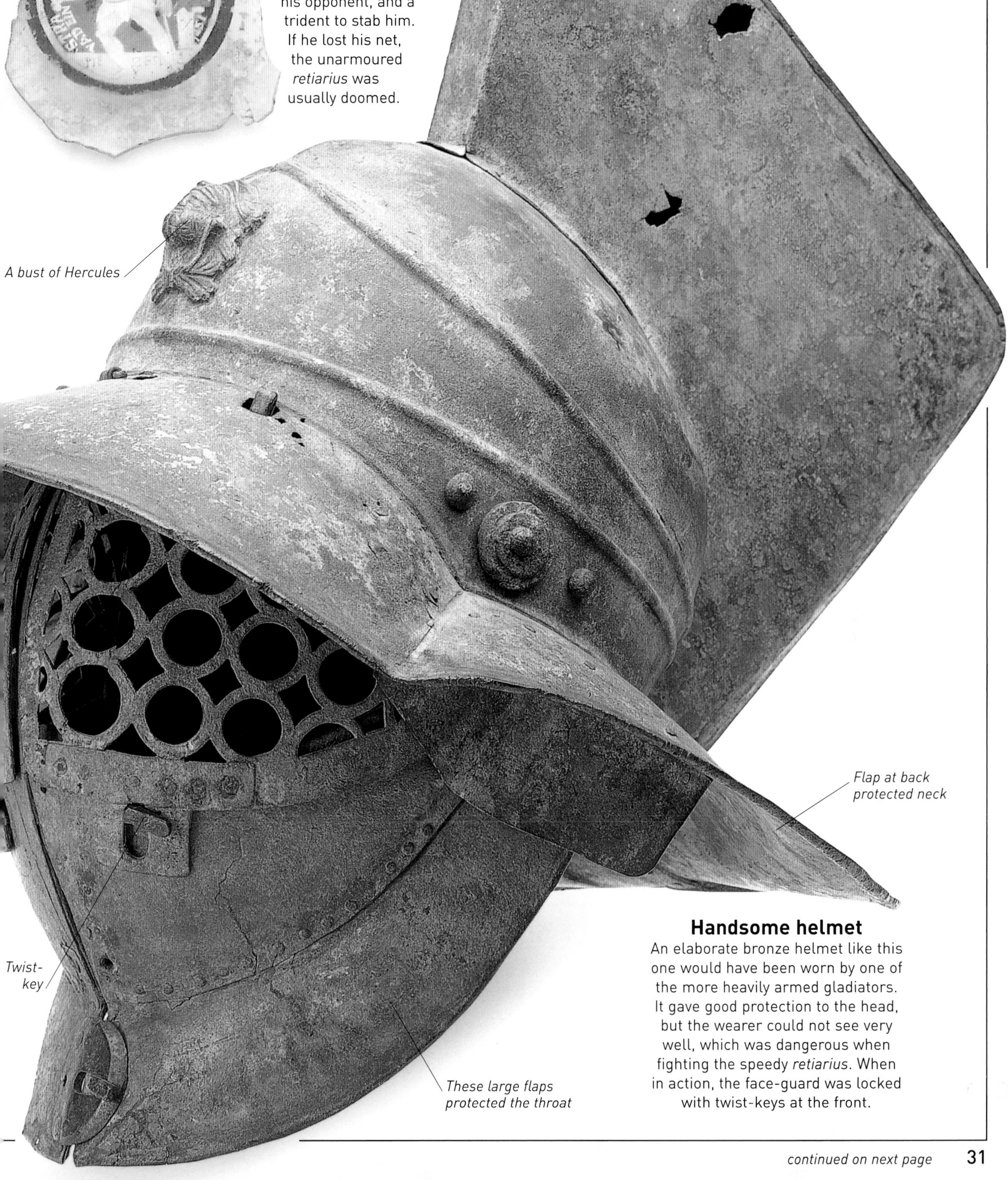

Decorative bronze crest

A bust of Hercules

Flap at back protected neck

Twist-key

These large flaps protected the throat

Handsome helmet

An elaborate bronze helmet like this one would have been worn by one of the more heavily armed gladiators. It gave good protection to the head, but the wearer could not see very well, which was dangerous when fighting the speedy *retiarius*. When in action, the face-guard was locked with twist-keys at the front.

continued on next page

Steel and claws

The games in the amphitheater lasted all day. In the morning, wild animals were brought on to fight each other or to face "huntsmen," or simply to kill defenseless criminals. Around noon there would be a break for the bodies to be removed while the crowd waited for the main attraction in the afternoon: the gladiators.

Bound for death
All kinds of animals from foreign lands, like this antelope, were captured and put on ships bound for Rome and the Colosseum. It was so important to the emperors to put on lavish spectacles that they spent vast sums of money on this cruel trade.

Elephant
In their endless search for novelty in the arena, the Romans scoured the known world for exotic animals like this African elephant.

Unprotected shoulder

Leopard is lunging at protected part of arm

"The brute tamer of Pompeii"
This 19th-century lion-tamer wore a "Roman" costume for his circus act.

Bear
Bears were found locally, but animals such as tigers, polar bears, ostriches, and rhinos had to be shipped in from farther afield.

Surprise attack
This clay plaque shows a leopard springing at an unwary *bestiarius* (animal fighter). Some of the huntsmen liked to show off, for example, fighting big cats while on stilts.

Deadly designs

The holes in this gladiator's face guard were small enough to protect the face without blocking the view. If the wearer was killed, the valuable armor was repaired and passed to another man.

The final moment

The last tense moment of a fight is shown on this oil lamp. A wounded gladiator waits for the victor to deliver the final blow.

Curved dagger

A life in the balance

A bronze statuette of one of the heavily armed gladiators shows the armor on his head, arms, legs, and unprotected stomach. He is probably wounded and appears to be raising his left hand to ask to be spared.

Shoulder guard to protect the neck

Lightly armed

Some gladiators were lightly armed, as shown in these bronze figures (above). On the left is a Thracian carrying a curved dagger; on the right is a *retiarius* (p.31).

The gladiators

"We who are about to die salute you," shouted the gladiators to the emperor, and the fighting began. Several pairs or groups fought at a time. When a gladiator was wounded he could appeal for mercy. The emperor listened to the crowd's opinion; had he fought well enough to be spared? If not, the people jabbed downward with their thumbs, and he was killed.

Duel to the death

This clay plaque shows two heavily armed gladiators. One thrusts at his opponent's neck; the other attacks the unprotected stomach.

Screen gladiator

Movies such as *Gladiator* (above) brought the terror of gladiator fights back to life. Here, actor Russell Crowe plays General Maximus, who fights to survive in the arena.

A day at the races

All over the Roman Empire, people flocked to see the "races". A day at the races meant a day spent betting on teams, cheering, and buying snacks from vendors. In an atmosphere charged with excitement, chariots creaked and horses stamped in the starting boxes. At the drop of a white cloth, the starting signal, the gates flew open, and they were off in a cloud of dust, thundering around the *spina*, or central barrier. The spectators went wild, cheering on their chosen team. In the capital, the four teams were called the Blues, Greens, Reds, and Whites.

Spectators
This mosaic shows people watching the races. Here, men and women could sit together, unlike at the gladiatorial and theatrical shows.

Victor
The winning charioteer received a victor's palm and a purse of gold.

Ben Hur
The film *Ben Hur* captured the excitement of a charioteer's life. Controlling four horses at full gallop was quite a task, especially at the turns.

Chariots were very light for maximum speed

Chariot and horse
Chariots called *bigae* were pulled by two horses; *quadrigae* had four horses. This bronze model is of a *biga* (one of the horses is missing). Races consisted of up to 12 chariots running seven laps, a total of about 8 km (5 miles). There were frequent crashes and deaths, but they just added to the excitement of the racegoers.

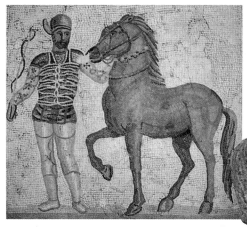

One man and his horse
This charioteer from the Blues team wears a leather harness to protect him in a fall. Successful charioteers often became very famous, and although mostly slaves, they sometimes made enough money to buy their freedom.

Ram's head finial on top of chariot pole

Champion stallions were used for breeding during their racing years

Bronze pole end
This chariot pole decoration shows a figure of a Triton (merman). Chariots were built for looks as well as speed.

The Triton blows a seashell trumpet

Reconstructed racetrack
The Circus Maximus in Rome seated up to 250,000 people. The chariots thundered round in an anti-clockwise direction. Seven laps later, the survivors crossed the finish-line opposite the emperor's box.

The theatre

The Romans largely copied theatre from Greece. Plays were first put on as part of religious festivals, and were later paid for by the wealthy to gain popularity. Tickets were free – if you could get them. Roman audiences generally preferred comedies to tragedies. The stories involved kidnapped heiresses, foolish old men, and cunning slaves, and usually had a happy ending. The Romans also invented other types of theatre, such as mime and pantomime. Roman pantomime involved an actor dancing and miming a story from Greek legend to musical accompaniment.

Mosaic masks
Roman actors were always men – women could only appear in mimes. They wore elaborate masks like these seen in the mosaic above. The masks told the audience what kind of character the actor was playing.

A comic actor
The scheming slave was a common figure in Roman comedy. When his plans were found out, he often ended up taking refuge on the altar in a temple, like the bronze figure above.

Tragic face
On the left is a marble carving of a female tragic mask. Actual masks were probably made of stiffened linen. There were gaping holes for the eyes and mouth.

A troupe of players
This mosaic, now in Naples, Italy, shows a group of actors dancing and playing musical instruments (p.48). The piper, wearing a white mask, is playing a female character.

A Roman theatre
Roman theatres were usually open to the sky. This one at Orange, in France, could hold 9,000 people. The wall behind the stage once had 76 decorative columns and many statues. It also had three doors through which the actors made their entrances.

Behind the scenes
This mosaic shows a group of Greek actors rehearsing a play. Two actors are practising their dance steps, while another is being helped into his costume. A musician plays the double pipes, and masks lie ready to be put on.

Bag of money

Dagger

Lamp

Unlike Roman actors, mimes did not wear masks

Figure holding a dagger

The classic symbol of theatre: tragic and comic masks

Figure holding a bag of money

Figure holding a lamp

Three mimes
These terracotta figures show a group of mimes performing a play. Roman mime was very different from modern mime because the actors spoke. It was also different from other Roman stage shows, because it was often performed on rough wooden stages set up in the streets. The actors did not wear masks, and women played female roles. Mime had regular comic figures, such as *Stupidus,* the fool.

The public baths

Few Roman houses had their own bathrooms; most people went to large public baths. These were not just places to get clean. Men went to the baths to meet friends, play games, and exercise. Women had separate baths, or went in the morning. Changing rooms, with shelves for clothes, led to rooms that got steadily hotter. The idea was to clean the pores of the skin by sweating. Soap was a foreign curiosity; olive oil was used instead. Afterward, there were cold plunge-baths to close the pores.

Ivory board-game counters

The inscription above means "bad luck"

Ivory (above), bone (above right), and glass counters

Agate dice

Rock crystal dice

Metal dice shaped like squatting men

Foundations
These foundations of a bathhouse were discovered in London, England, in 1989. You can see the bottoms of the brick pillars that once supported the raised floor.

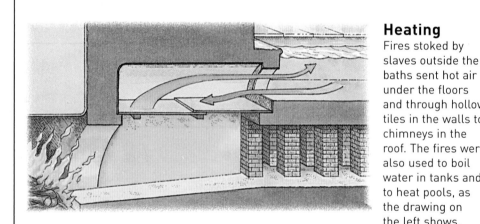

Heating
Fires stoked by slaves outside the baths sent hot air under the floors and through hollow tiles in the walls to chimneys in the roof. The fires were also used to boil water in tanks and to heat pools, as the drawing on the left shows.

Games

People came to the baths to exercise and play in the yard, some perhaps training with weights, others playing ball games. These included catching games, which were played with colored balls of all sizes, including heavy medicine balls. The less energetic bought drinks and snacks from vendors, or sat in the shade playing board games, or gambling with dice.

Hot springs at Bath
The Romans used the natural hot springs at Bath, England, as part of a medical center. Sick people came from all over the country to seek a cure by swimming in the waters.

Colored glass counters for a board game

Bath tools
This 19th-century painting by Sir Lawrence Alma-Tadema shows Roman women cleaning themselves with sponges and strigils (tools for scraping the oil and dirt from the skin).

Ear-scoop

Nail cleaner

Tweezers

Toilet set
This bronze pocket toilet set from London includes useful tools for personal hygiene.

Slot for hanging or attaching to a carrying handle (above right)

A cold splash
Dishes, or *paterae*, like the bronze example (left), were used for splashing cold water over the body to close the pores after the heat of the baths.

Base of patera *has worn away over the centuries*

Handle for hanging cleaning implements from

Detachable lid of oil flask

All set for the baths
This set of utensils would leave you well equipped for a visit to the baths. The oil flask, and the pair of strigils are attached to a carrying handle. This was like a large key-ring, allowing the tools to be easily removed.

Curved part of strigil was used for scraping off dirt

Oil flask
This second-century CE oil flask from Britain is decorated with three African faces.

Writing it all down

Many different languages were spoken across the Roman Empire, but Latin was the main language used for trade, government, and communication. The Romans introduced writing to northern Europe, and the Latin alphabet is still widely used today. There were only 22 letters in the alphabet (I and J, and U and V, were not distinguished, and V and W did not exist). Millions of texts were written, from private letters scrawled on wax tablets to elegant poems written in ink on papyrus scrolls. Books, however, were rare and expensive because they had to be copied by hand.

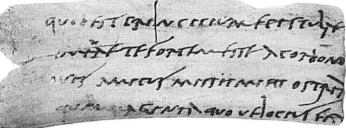

Roman handwriting
This is a fragment of a Latin letter, written in ink on a wooden tablet. It was discovered at the fort of Vindolanda near Hadrian's Wall in England. Addressed to a soldier named Lucius, it is about a welcome gift of oysters from a friend of the writer.

Trajan's Column
The inscription on the base of Trajan's Column in Rome is a famous example of beautifully proportioned Roman capitals, which were often painted on walls or carved into stone.

Sooty ink
Soot was mixed with water to make ink.

Roman numerals
Roman numerals were written as strings of symbols to be added together, with I for 1, V for 5, X for 10, C for 100, and so on. Large numbers were very clumsy and complicated, for example 1,778 in Roman numerals is MDCCLXXVIII.

Waxing lyrical
Melted beeswax was poured into wooden frames to make a reusable writing surface.

The number four can be IV or IIII

Roman numerals are still used on modern clocks and watches

Vellum

Egyptian inkpot
This inkpot dating to the first century CE, is made of faience (a glassy material).

Writers

These portraits from Pompeii show a woman with a wax tablet and a stylus, and a man with a papyrus scroll. The tablet has two leaves that folded together to protect the writing.

Inlaid inkpots

On the left is a bronze inkpot with a silver inlay and a lid to stop the ink from drying up. Below is a pair of bronze inkpots, covered with black niello (silver or copper sulfide) and inlaid with silver and gold. It is decorated with mythological scenes.

Reed pen with split nib

Bronze pen

Bronze stylus from Athens

Spatula for smoothing the wax to erase writing

Iron stylus with bronze cover

Ivory stylus

Hanging inkpot

This inkpot once had cords to hang it up or to carry it.

Tools

Split-nib pens were used with ink to write on papyrus, wood, or vellum. The pointed stylus was designed for writing on wax tablets.

Papyrus

Papyrus and vellum

Important documents were written on Egyptian papyrus (paper made from reeds). The finest books were written on long-lasting vellum, made from sheets of wafer-thin animal skin.

Crafts and technology

The Romans were highly skilled at working in all sorts of materials, from leather, textiles, and wood, to metal and glass. Pottery was a huge industry in some areas, where wine jars (p.60) and red Samian pots (p.47) were made by the million in large workshops. Other crafts were on a much smaller scale, with individual artisans working from their own shops in towns like Pompeii. Many of the potters were slaves or freedmen. Surviving names show that they, and other craftsmen, were almost all men.

Teardrop-shaped decoration on beaker

Face

Face flask
This mass-produced flask was made by blowing a bubble of glass into a mould.

Moulded beaker
The mould for this glass beaker had the teardrop decoration on the inside.

Glassworking

Glass had been made for centuries, but in the last century BCE someone had discovered that it was possible to blow glass into bubbles. Soon glass was being blown into moulds, allowing mass production of bottles and highly decorated flasks. Glass was no longer just a luxury, but became a widely used material.

Blue ribbed bowl
This bowl is made of expensive blue glass. It was probably made using the older technique of pressing hot glass into a mould.

Portland Vase
The Portland Vase is one of the most precious objects to survive from Roman times. Using a highly skilled technique called cameo carving, the jeweller covered the blue glass with a layer of white glass. He then cut away the white layer to leave the elegant figures and foliage on the blue background.

Glass jar

Lid of jar

Bands of gold running through the glass

Colourful glass
Some vessels, like this delicate little jar and lid, contained bands of coloured glass and even gold. The jar was probably used for storing some expensive cosmetic (p.18).

Metalwork

Gold, silver, lead, copper, iron, and other metals were widely used by the Romans. Blacksmiths could not make furnaces hot enough to melt iron, so they hammered it into shape while it was hot. To make bronze, they mixed copper with tin. Roman bronze often had zinc in it as well, giving it a gold colour.

Silver mirror
Mirror glass was not yet invented in Roman times, so polished metal was used instead.

Outline of figure which was originally inlaid with gold foil

Curved blade of knife

Bronze plaque
This small sheet of bronze bears a delicate gold foil inlay set into its surface.

Smith's tools
These iron tongs were used to heat small metal objects in a furnace.

This iron file has lost its wooden handle

Jeweller's hoard
These silver objects are part of a large hoard of jewellery, coins, and scrap silver that was buried at Snettisham, England, in the second century CE.

Recycling
Fragments of old jewellery were melted down to make new items.

Silver ingot

Boneworking

Bone was used for making many everyday items, such as knife handles, hairpins, and combs. Fresh animal bone from the butcher's could be quite finely carved, and was used for inlays on wooden boxes. Gaming counters and dice were also carved from bone (p.38).

Woman's head on end of hairpin

Bone pins
Large needles and pins were usually made from bone. Hairpins were necessary for the elaborate hairstyles worn by Roman women (p.19).

Bone handle
Roman knives often had a carved bone handle and a hanging-loop.

Loop for hanging knife

Bone comb
The comb's teeth were cut with a very fine saw.

Rings
There were 89 rings in the hoard, some with gems.

Silver pendant for attaching to a necklace

This shaped stone found with the hoard is a polishing tool

In the kitchen

Roman cooking might seem strange to us today—one common recipe involved cooking dormice in honey. Many of today's basic foods were not yet known. The Romans had no potatoes or tomatoes, and pasta had not yet been invented. Ordinary people ate simple foods, such as bread, beans, lentils, and a little meat. Even wealthier Romans ate very little during the day. The main meal was dinner (p.46). Larger houses had chefs who made complicated dishes with herbs and sauces. The look of the food was as important as the taste.

Mice like these robbed many a Roman kitchen

Grater
This modern-looking bronze grater was probably used for preparing cheese and vegetables.

Cook's knife
Sharp knives were needed to carve meat.

Wooden spoon
Wooden spoons, such as this one from Egypt, would have been found in almost every Roman kitchen.

Lip in mortarium *for pouring out finished product*

Market fare
This mosaic from Rome shows fish, poultry, and vegetables. Fresh fish was too expensive for most ordinary Romans.

Mortar and pestle
The *mortarium*, or grinding dish, was made of tough pottery with coarse grit in the surface. It was used with a pestle (seen inside the vessel) to grind foodstuffs into powders, pastes, or liquids.

Reusable bottle
Glass bottles were used for trading valuable liquids. When empty, they were used to store food in the kitchen.

Bronze saucepan

Many kitchen utensils were made from bronze. However, bronze contains copper, which can affect some types of food. The pan on the left has been coated with silver and tin to prevent this.

Bronze strainer

Roman cooks used strainers like this one to drain boiled food, and to separate juices and sauces.

Utensil was hung up on kitchen wall by this hole

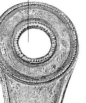

A Roman kitchen

This Pompeii kitchen scene shows a stove, with bronze pans still on the surface (p.57). Roman stoves were fueled by wood or charcoal.

Celery was a popular vegetable in Rome

A bun pan?

This interesting utensil might have been used for baking buns or for poaching eggs.

Thyme

Coriander seeds

Juniper berries

Pepper

The Romans used a variety of herbs in cooking, easily grown in the warm climate

Rue

Oregano

Fish sauce

A popular ingredient in Roman cuisine was *garum*, a strong-tasting sauce made from fish, salt, and other ingredients. *Garum*, like olive oil and wine, was traded in *amphorae* (p.60).

A Mediterranean fish such as this one would have been used to make *garum*

A dinner party

After a day's work, which started at dawn, and a visit to the baths (p.38), the well-to-do Roman went home for the main meal of the day. Dinner (*cena*) normally started at two or three in the afternoon and lasted all evening. It was often more of a social event than a leisurely meal. There were frequently guests, with entertainment from clowns, dancers, or musicians between courses. People ate reclining on large couches that held up to three people. The couches were placed around three sides of a low table. The fourth side was left open so that slaves had room to serve the family and their guests.

18th-century drawing of a Roman dancer with grapes

Glass bowl
The rich adorned their tables with fine glassware, Besides being beautiful, glass was popular because it was easier to clean than most pottery.

Roman wine
There were many varieties of Roman wine, both dry and sweet. The Romans drank their wine mixed with water, and sometimes added flavors such as honey.

Wine was usually mixed with water, so was probably light in color

White swirling design in glass

Delicate patterns on side of cup

Bronze pitcher
Pitchers for wine and water were made from pottery, glass, bronze, or silver.

A feast
This detail, from a 19th-century painting by Edward A. Armitage, gives an impression of what a Roman banquet would have looked like.

Wine cups
Decorated with graceful floral scrolls, birds, and insects, these beautiful silver cups originally had stems and feet.

Samian pottery

Glossy red pottery called Samian ware was very fashionable in the first and second centuries CE. Millions of these pitchers, platters, bowls, and cups were made in factories in Italy and Gaul, and were shipped all over the Empire. They were elegant, easy to keep clean, and designed to stack for easy transport and storage. A crate of Samian ware was found during the excavations at Pompeii (p.57). It had just been delivered from Gaul and had not even been unpacked.

Samian platter with grapes

Samian wine pitcher

The dish is modern

The Romans usually had fresh fruit for dessert, including figs

Samian cup

Asparagus tips for decoration

Olives, widely grown in the Mediterranean regions, were probably eaten as appetizers, just as they are today

Songbird surprise

On the right is a reproduction of an actual Roman dish from an original recipe. It consists of small songbirds served with an asparagus sauce and quail's eggs. The birds (in this case quails) would probably have been carefully arranged on a platter like this to delight and impress the host's guests.

Making music

Music, song, and dance were popular with the Roman people. Music was played in the theatre and at private parties. It also accompanied religious ceremonies and other public events like gladiatorial shows. Many Roman instruments were of Greek origin, like the lyre (far right). The most common instruments were wind instrumentsm, such as reed pipes and bronze horns. These produced loud notes which could be heard easily at outside events. The most complicated Roman instrument was the water organ, invented by a Greek in the third century BCE. It used a pump to force water into a closed chamber, and produced notes or chords like a modern organ.

Pan
The statuette above shows the god Pan (p.51) holding a set of pan-pipes. The instrument was made up of a row of cane whistles of different lengths.

Music and dance
This mosaic shows a woman with castanets dancing to music played on the double pipes. Bands of performers, like these, played in the streets, or were hired to appear at dinner parties.

Frenzied dance
Music and dance were important parts of worship in some religions. The dancers seen on the stone relief above are probably followers of the goddess Isis (p.50). They are working themselves into a state of frenzied joy by the movements of the dance.

Rodent rhythm
This comic figurine shows a musical rat or mouse playing a bronze horn.

Double trouble
A bronze satyr (woodland god) plays the double pipes (a pair of simple flutes). There is no modern instrument like them. They must have been very difficult to learn to play – both flutes had to be blown at the same time.

Spiral horn

The cornu was a very long horn curved into a spiral. It was often used in the army for signalling, and for music at ceremonies.

Bronze figure decorates mouthpiece

Musical god

This fresco shows the sun god Apollo holding a lyre. He was also the patron of music and poetry.

Flute

Like a modern flute, this Roman example was played by blowing across a hole. It has been restored from damaged fragments, probably incorrectly, and can no longer be played.

Hole for leather or cord straps

Finger holes, covered to achieve different notes

Bronze cymbals

These bronze cymbals were found at Praeneste in Italy. Other Roman percussion instruments included the *sistrum* (a metal rattle used for religious purposes) and simple tambourine-like drums.

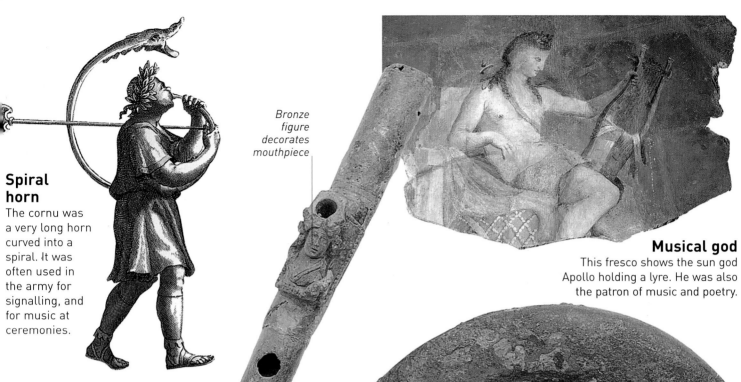

Roman gods

The Roman people worshipped hundreds of different gods and goddesses. Everyone was expected to make sacrifices to the most important Roman gods, such as Jupiter, the protector of the Roman Empire. They also worshipped past emperors, who were often made into gods when they died. The Romans believed that the gods watched over every part of their lives. There were gods to protect the house (p.23), gods of war, and gods of healing. Some worshipped foreign gods, such as Mithras or Isis, who offered hope in the afterlife.

Peacock sits on Juno's throne

God of thunder
The king of the Roman gods was Jupiter, a sky-god whose symbols were the eagle and the thunderbolt. His temple stood on the Capitoline Hill in Rome.

Juno
The wife of Jupiter, Juno, was the patron goddess of women. Her symbol was a peacock.

Imperial temple
Most emperors were declared gods after their deaths, and temples were built to worship them. This well-preserved temple in Vienne, France, was built to honour Emperor Augustus and his wife Livia (p.9) who were both made into gods. Offerings were made at an altar in front of the building (p.52).

Egyptian gods
Some Romans worshipped foreign gods, as well as their own gods. The Egyptian goddess Isis (left) and the god Serapis (above) were among the most popular. Their religion was about the cycle of life, death, and rebirth.

War goddess
Minerva, the goddess of war, is shown here with her helmet and armour. She was also the goddess of handicrafts and wisdom.

Mars and Venus

Mars, the god of war, is still remembered in the name of the month, March. Gauls and Britons based many of their own gods on Roman ones. The silver plaque from Britain on the right is dedicated to a Roman-British god called Mars Alator. Venus, the Roman goddess of love, was said to be a divine ancestor of Julius Caesar.

Inscription says that the plaque was given to fulfil a promise to the god

Bronze statue of the goddess Venus

Persian god

This marble statue shows the Persian god Mithras killing a sacred bull. The bull's blood was thought to give life to the universe.

A riotous god

Bacchus was the Roman name for the Greek god Dionysus, the god of wine and rebirth.

Bacchus holds grapes as a symbol of wine

Busts of gods decorate this clamp used in religious ceremonies

Cybele

Cybele was a Turkish goddess. Her religion was about the cycle of death and rebirth. It was a very emotional religion, and sometimes her priests would work themselves into a frenzy.

The monster is eating a man

Goat god

One of many Greek gods adopted by Rome, Pan was half-man, half-goat. He was a god of shepherds and mountains could cause herds of animals to "panic" and stampede.

Celtic god

The Britons and Gauls believed in some grim gods, like this monster.

Priests and worship

The Romans feared the gods, and wanted to win their favour. People would pray and make offerings at temples to ask for divine favours or to give thanks. These offerings came in all shapes and sizes, from coins and brooches left by the poor, to silver statues donated by the rich. People also sacrificed food and drink, and burnt incense on altars. Animal sacrifices were common, ranging from a single bird to a whole herd of cattle. There were few full-time priests or priestesses, except for the Vestal Virgins, who guarded the holy flame of the goddess Vesta in Rome.

Priestess
A priestess pours a libation (offering) of milk, oil, or wine onto the altar of a god or goddess. The cults of Vesta, Isis, and Cybele were particularly associated with women.

Libation jug
A bronze jug such as this one (right) was used for holding liquids to pour in sacrifices.

Lion-headed handle

Under the knife
Animals were sacrificed in various ways; large beasts like cattle were felled with an axe. Then a knife was used to cut the animal open.

Libation bowl
A libation bowl was used to pour liquids into the fire on the altar. The smoke would then rise to the heavens to please the god.

Curse tablet

People would seek revenge on their enemies by placing a curse on them. This lead plaque from the temple at Uley in England, asks Mercury to make the thieves who stole a valuable animal fall sick until they return it.

Bones

Certain animals were chosen to be sacrificed to particular gods. Mercury's "holy animals" were the cock and the ram. Bones found at Uley show that chickens and sheep were also sacrificed in his honour.

Offering a sacrifice

On this relief from Italy, a Silenus (Greek woodland spirit) is shown making an offering at an altar. Sileni were companions of the god Bacchus (p.51).

Divine messenger

Above is a little bronze statue of Mercury, the messenger of the gods. It was left as an offering at his temple at Uley.

Animal liver

This marble hand is holding an animal's liver. A special priest would read the god's will from the liver's shape. It was thought to be bad news if the organ was damaged.

The way the sacred chickens ate showed whether the gods approved of a plan

Sacrificial altar

Roman altars stood in the open, at the front of the temple.

Boar to the slaughter

A boar is led to the altar for sacrifice. Its inner organs were burnt as offerings to the gods; the good meat was cooked and eaten.

Healing the sick

The causes of disease were not well understood in Roman times. Many Romans believed that illness was caused by the gods, curses, or witchcraft. Some people wore magic charms to ward off disease; others visited healing shrines to pray to the gods. The sick took herbal medicines or traveled to healing centers such as Bath in England (p.38). Roman doctors had some effective drugs, but with no real anesthetics, surgery was agonizing and dangerous.

Signet rings

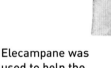

The rings above show Aesculapius (the god of healing) and Hygeia, who symbolized health. The rings were probably worn to ward off illness.

Clay Ear

When asking a god for a cure, people often left a model of the injured part of the body at the temple.

Bronze leg

This bronze leg was dedicated to a god by a man named Caledus.

Physician and child

This marble tombstone (left) shows a Greek doctor examining a child. On the ground lies an outsize "cupping vessel" used for extracting blood.

Elecampane was used to help the digestion

Fenugreek was used for treating pneumonia

Healing herbs

Many plant materials were known to have healing properties.

Sage, a powerful healer, was sacred to the Romans

Fennel was thought to have calming properties

Rosemary was widely used in Roman medicine

The Roman writer Pliny listed 40 remedies with mustard as the main ingredient

Soldiers were given a daily ration of garlic for health

Insula Tiberina

After a plague in the third century BCE, the Romans built a temple to the god Aesculapius on a small island in the Tiber River. It remained a center of healing right into medieval times.

The saw has lost its handle

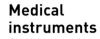

Medical instruments

On this page is a range of medical instruments used by Roman doctors. Most of the tools were made of bronze.

A spoon for giving liquid medicines

Decorative handle of probe

Saw and forceps

The saw above was used for cutting bones. Tweezerlike forceps (left) were used to remove splinters or fragments of tissue.

Scalpel

End of bronze catheter

Folding knife

Ouch!

The wall painting below shows the legendary hero Aeneas having an arrow-head removed from his thigh with forceps.

Speculum

This device was used for internal examinations.

Probe

Before operations, probes like the one on the left were used to explore the wound.

Handle of speculum

Hooks

These hooks were used for holding blood vessels and other body parts out of the way during operations.

Catheter

Fine bronze curved tubes like this were used for draining the bladder.

Central pivot

Squeezing the handles together (right) opened these prongs

Spatula for mixing and applying ointments

Burial rites

Life expectancy for Romans was generally short. This was due to poor diet, a lack of medical care, and hard living conditions. Children were particularly at risk, with up to one in three dying young. It is likely that less than half of the population survived to the age of 50, although a few lived to their 80s and beyond. Over time, funeral customs changed. Instead of cremating (burning) bodies, more people chose to bury their loved ones.

In the catacombs
In Rome, Christians buried their dead in catacombs – a series of underground tunnels and chambers with gaps in the walls for coffins. Funeral services were held in the underground chapels.

Marble urn
After a body was cremated, the ashes were put in containers called urns and placed in family tombs. The inscription on this carved marble urn tells us that it belongs to a woman called Bovia Procula, a "most unfortunate mother". She may have died in childbirth.

Remembering Avita
The tombstone above is that of a 10-year-old girl called Avita, shown as her parents wanted to remember her, with her books and her pet dog.

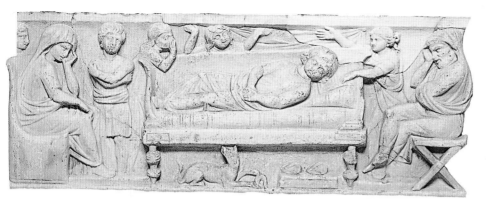

Across the River Styx

This marble carving shows a child on her deathbed, surrounded by her grieving relatives. The Romans believed that the dead were ferried across the River Styx to Hades (the Underworld), and so they often put a coin in the mouth of the body to pay the ferryman. The funeral would involve a solemn procession to the cemetery for burial, or to the place of cremation.

Street of tombs

Roman cemeteries were built outside the town gates. The best burial spots were next to the road, where passers-by could see the graves. Remembering the dead, especially the family ancestors, was very important to the Romans.

Buried under ash

In 79 CE, Mount Vesuvius erupted without warning. Burning rocks and ash from the volcano rained over the surrounding areas, burying everything up to 4 m (13 ft) deep. The nearby city of Pompeii was frozen in time by a deep blanket of ash and rock. Life ended so suddenly in Pompeii that we are able to learn a lot about the lives of the people there. Ash hardened around the victims' bodies, so that although the flesh has long since gone, hollow "moulds" of their original shapes can still be found.

Glass urn

The ashes of the dead were often put into pots and glass vessels like this urn.

Victim of Vesuvius

Above is the plaster cast of the "mould" of the body of a man found in Pompeii. The shape of his clothes and shoes are still visible. Many of the victims desperately tried to shield themselves from the ashes and fumes.

Fragments of burnt bone from the urn

Country life

Plowing the land
The bronze model above shows a British plowman at work with his team of cattle.

Most ordinary Romans lived in the countryside, working the land, rearing livestock, and growing crops. Farming was a backbreaking life of endless toil for men, women, and children, many of whom were slaves. Much of Italy was divided into huge farming estates owned by wealthy Romans. The rich liked to escape the heat of town in the summer, and retreated to their country estates where they owned fine houses (villas), with luxuries such as baths.

Reaping hook
Sickles like the one on the left were used for cutting grain.

Emmer
Roman farmers grew a variety of cereals, including emmer, an ancient type of wheat. It is shown here (left) both as ripened ears and as grain ready to make into bread and other foods.

Boar hunt
This mosaic from Sicily illustrates the dangers of boar hunting. The hunters are armed with spears and dogs.

The thrill of the chase
Roman huntsmen enjoyed the thrill of chasing the wild boar, with its great speed and razor-sharp tusks.

A Roman villa

This finely preserved wall-painting is from the villa of the empress Livia (p.9). Many wealthy Romans owned elegant country houses with shaded corridors, gardens, and pools.

Bronze bull

Roman farmers kept livestock for eating, dairy produce, and leather. Bulls, such as this splendid beast, were reared for breeding.

Sheep shears

Iron shears like these were used for shearing sheep.

The modern drawing above shows Cupids (gods of love) picking and treading grapes

Winemaking

Grapes and olives were important crops in sunny Mediterranean lands like Italy. Olive oil was used in cooking and bathing (p.38), and was exported across the Empire. Grapes were cultivated for winemaking, which was already an ancient art in Roman times. Wine, mixed with water, was the most popular drink in Roman times (p.46).

Glass "grape" flask

Shepherd boy

This lovely silver figurine of a shepherd boy portrays a very romantic view of country life.

Lamb peeping out of shepherd's shoulder bag

Nile landscape

This mosaic, from Pompeii, shows the variety of wildlife that could be hunted along the River Nile in Egypt.

Bronze goat

Goats provided milk, cheese, and meat.

Trade and travel

In the first and second centuries CE, there was a long period of peace known as the *Pax Romana* (Roman Peace). During this time, the Roman Empire became rich and prosperous. The army built a vast network of roads that helped open up the Empire. Merchant ships carried goods such as wine and olive oil to Britain and Gaul, while grain was brought across from North Africa. Soldiers, politicians, and even some tourists traveled across the Empire, and with them spread new fashions and ideas. During this time, Christianity spread from the east, along the roads and seaways, to the cities of the west.

Bronze donkey
Animals such as donkeys were used for transporting goods. They pulled carts and wagons, or carried loads on their backs.

Storage vessels
These pottery jars, called *amphorae*, held Italian wine, mostly for selling to other countries. Their shape allowed them to be tightly packed together in the holds of merchant ships.

Dupondius

As

Aureus

Sestertius

Denarius

Ready money
Coins were minted by the emperor mainly to pay the soldiers and to collect taxes. Almost everyone across the Empire used these coins, which made trading simpler.

Trade ship
A marble relief from Carthage shows a small trading boat and its helmsman. In the summer, ships laden with goods sailed as far as Britain and India. The seas were dangerous in winter, and many boats did not sail during the colder months.

This weight allowed the balance to work rather like a steelyard

Bronze scales
Roman traders used two common types of scales for weighing goods: simple bronze balances like this, and another type called a steelyard (below).

A steelyard for weighing the meat

The chains are modern replacements

The pans could be lifted off the hooks and bags used instead

The butcher's
A stone relief shows a butcher at work with a cleaver, while his customer sits and waits for her goods. Joints of meat can be seen hanging from the rail above.

Hook for weighing bags

Steelyard
The item to be weighed was attached to the lower hook on the left, and the weight on the right was moved along until the arm balanced horizontally. The item's weight could then be read from a scale written on the arm.

The weight is shaped like an acorn

Official weight
This bronze weight from Turkey is decorated with a bust of Hercules. Weights were checked by officials to stop traders from cheating.

The twilight of Rome

Great changes overcame the Roman Empire after 200 CE. There were constant clashes with the "barbarians" to the north, and the Persians to the east. Frequent civil wars broke out as generals once more struggled for power. Finally, Diocletian and his three co-emperors managed to restore peace, dividing the Empire into two parts – east and west. One of Diocletian's successors, Constantine, believed that he came to power with the help of the Christian god. By his death, in 337 CE, Christianity had become the new state religion.

A Christian family
This fragment of gold glass depicts a family with the early Christian symbol "Chi-Rho" (from the first two letters of Christ's name in Greek).

Latin west
Below (left) is a silver statuette representing Rome, the old pagan, western capital.

The 30 pieces of silver paid to Judas for his betrayal

Christ on the cross
This ivory box from about 420 CE depicts the crucifixion of Christ, and, on the left, Judas hanging himself.

The baptism of Constantine, the first Christian emperor

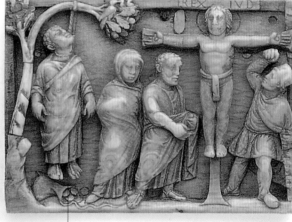

The decline of the west

As Christianity triumphed, the western Empire was beginning to break up as Germanic invaders poured into the Empire. In 410 CE, Rome was sacked, and in 476 CE, the last western emperor lost his power. Rome had fallen, but the eastern Empire lived on.

Greek east
Above (right) is a representation of Constantinople, the new eastern capital and Christian city founded by Constantine. Today it is called Istanbul.

Brooches

Many of the Germanic invaders were skilled craftsmen who made spectacular jewellery. The brooches on the left were made by the Ostrogoths in about 500 CE, from silver, gold, green glass, and red garnet.

Red garnet inlaid in the gold

Iron spearhead

Two iron arrowheads

Weapons of war

This iron spearhead and two arrowheads come from the grave of one of the Frankish conquerors of Gaul. By the time these were buried in the sixth century CE, the new Frankish kingdom had been established.

Barbarians

When the "barbarian" peoples burst into the western Empire in the fourth century CE, they founded many of the states of modern Europe; the Franks turned Gaul into France, while the Angles and Saxons turned Roman Britain into Saxon England.

Attila the Hun

The Huns from central Asia devastated Europe in the fifth century CE. The Pope (right) is shown negotiating with their leader Attila in 452 CE. It was thought that this saved Rome from further destruction.

The east survives

The eastern Empire also came under attack, but it survived until 1453. This Greek-speaking Christian state was very different from old Rome, and went on to become the Byzantine Empire.

Artemis, the Greek goddess of hunting

Byzantine emperor

The steelyard weight (p.61) on the right depicts a seventh-century Byzantine emperor. He looks more like a medieval king than a Roman emperor.

Medallion

The Christian Byzantines respected their Greek and Roman heritage, and sometimes still used pagan images, such as the figure on this sixth-century gold medallion.

Did you know?

FASCINATING FACTS

Romans washed their dishes by rubbing them with sand, then rinsing them in clean water.

The Romans believed that a goddess of chance, called Fortuna, controlled their lives. Since she was permanently blindfolded, her decisions were made at random.

The goddess Fortuna

Fontana della Fortuna in Fano, Italy

On his journey over the Alps to invade Rome in 218 BCE, the Carthaginian general Hannibal lost 14,000 men and 25 elephants.

The names of all our months have Roman origins: August honours the emperor Augustus, while March is named after Mars, the god of war.

At the Colosseum in ancient Rome, up to 5,000 pairs of gladiators fought and 5,000 animals could be killed during a single event.

To construct the outside walls of the Colosseum, it took 292,000 cartloads of travertine stone, carried along a specially-built road from Tivoli, in the hills outside Rome.

After the birth of Christianity, the events at the Colosseum declined in popularity, and large sections of the building were removed to provide construction materials for other projects. This was still happening in the Middle Ages.

If rebel Roman slaves were caught, they were crucified – nailed to a cross until they died. In a revolt led by Spartacus in 73 CE, 6,000 slaves were crucified.

In a Roman household, the father had absolute power: he could even condemn his wife, his children, and any of their slaves to death if he felt they deserved it.

The language of ancient Rome was Latin, but many of the people ruled by the Romans had their own languages or dialects. The Oscans, for example, who lived in Campania (the area around Naples), had their own distinctive script.

Ornamental bust of Hercules

Gladiator's helmet

One emperor, the mad Caligula (37–41 CE), tried to have his horse appointed as a senator.

When Mount Vesuvius erupted in 79 CE, it buried the seaside town of Herculaneum under 20 m (66 ft) of ash and debris.

Painting showing the eruption of Mount Vesuvius

As well as military training, legionaries in the Roman army were given instruction in surveying, engineering, and building, so they could construct camps, forts, and defensive walls.

The Roman culture and civilization owed a great deal to those of ancient Greece. The Romans worshipped many of the same gods as the Greeks, they developed their alphabet from the Greek one, and much of their art, literature, and theatre was based on Greek models.

Many of the works of Roman writers and philosophers are still widely read today. If it were not for the teams of medieval monks who painstakingly copied out and illustrated them, however, many of these texts would have been lost forever.

QUESTIONS AND ANSWERS

Q How do we know so much about ancient Rome?

A Experts have learned a great deal from existing Roman buildings and artefacts. Information about politics, history, religion, and culture comes largely from Roman documents. Roman mosaics, sculpture, and paintings show us clearly what people and everyday objects looked like.

Q How different were Roman homes from modern ones?

A Roman houses had less furniture in them, and more decoration on the walls and floors, in the form of mosaics and wall-paintings. Much less primitive than you might imagine, the homes of the very rich even had running water, flushing toilets, and central heating.

Q Did the ancient Romans eat the same foods we eat?

A Many of the things they ate and drank would be familiar to us: bread, for example, eggs, fruit (such as apples, pears, figs, dates, plums, and grapes), vegetables (celery, carrots, cabbage, beans, and asparagus), and wine (usually diluted with water). The Romans ate less meat than us, but lamb and pork were popular. Fish, together with exotic birds like cranes, parrots, flamingoes and peacocks, provided special-occasion treats for the very rich.

Roman mosaic

Q What was life like for women in ancient Rome?

A Most Roman women were poorly educated. They could not vote or hold office, and few occupations were open to them. A woman's status depended on her husband, but she could also exert power through him: Livia, for example, the wife of Emperor Augustus, had no official role, yet it was widely accepted that she ruled alongside him.

18th-century engraving of a Roman woman

Record Breakers

Bust of Julius Caesar

- **ARCHITECTURAL TRIUMPH** The Pantheon temple in Rome, completed in 24 CE, has a huge dome that was the largest in existence until the 19th century. The Pantheon still stands today.

- **HEAD ON A COIN** The first living Roman to appear on a coin was Julius Caesar.

- **THRIVING METROPOLIS** Rome was the largest city in the Empire with a population of more than 1,000,000 in 1 CE.

- **RETAIL HEAVEN** The first-ever shopping mall was built by Emperor Trajan in Rome. Arranged over several levels, it contained more than 150 shopping outlets.

- **ROADS TO ROME** The Via Appia was the first road in a sophisticated network that eventually covered 96,500 km (60,000 miles) and connected Rome with all the important towns of the Empire.

- **GALLOPING INFLATION** In the 3rd century CE, prices in the Empire spiralled out of control. Between 200–280 CE, the cost of a bale of wheat in Egypt rose from 16 to 120,000 drachmas.

- **DETAILED HISTORY** The scholar Titus Livius (Livy) wrote a history of Rome that filled 142 books, 35 of which have survived. His works were used as textbooks in Roman schools.

Songbirds for supper

The emperors

After 500 years, civil war brought the period in Roman history known as the Republic to an end. Julius Caesar's adopted son Octavian became Rome's first emperor. He was given the name *Imperator Caesar Augustus*. The word *imperator* meant "victor in battle".

Emperors wore laurel wreaths

Augustus Caesar
Augustus was not only the first Roman emperor, he was also a great leader and administrator and an enlightened patron of literature and the arts. The period of his rule is known as the Augustan Age.

Gallic rebel states	
Postumus	260–269
Victorinus	269–271
Tetricus	271–274

Temporary rebellion
A period of foreign invasions and civil wars allowed the growth of rebel states: the kingdom of Palmyra in the east and the "Gallic Empire" of Gaul (France), Britain, and Spain. They were finally defeated by the emperor Aurelian.

Eastern rebel state of Palmyra	
Zenobia	266–272
(Joint ruler with her son Vaballath)	

Gallienus

Roman emperors	
Augustus	27 BCE–14 CE
Tiberius	14–37 CE
Caligula (Gauis)	37–41
Claudius	41–54
Nero	54–68
Galba	68–69
Otho	69
Vitellius	69
Vespasian	69–79
Titus	79–81
Domitian	81–96
Nerva	96–98
Trajan	98–117
Hadrian	117–138
Antoninus Pius	138–161
Marcus Aurelius	161–180
Lucius Verus (Co-emperor)	161–169
Commodus	177–192
Pertinax	193
Didius Julianus	193
Septimius Severus	193–211
Caracalla	211–217
Geta	211–212
Macrinus	217–218
Elagabalus	218–222
Alexander Severus	222–235
Maximinus I	235–238
Gordian	238
Gordian II	238
Pupienus	238
Balbinus	238
Gordian III	238–244
Philip	244–249
Decius	249–251
Hostilian	251
Gallus	251–253
Aemilianus	253
Gallienus	253–268
Valerian	253–260
Claudius II Gothicus	268–270
Quintillus	270
Aurelian	270–275
Tacitus	275–276
Florianus	276
Probus	276–282
Carus	282–283
Carinus	283–284
Numerianus (Co-emperor)	283–284
Diocletian	284–305

Claudius

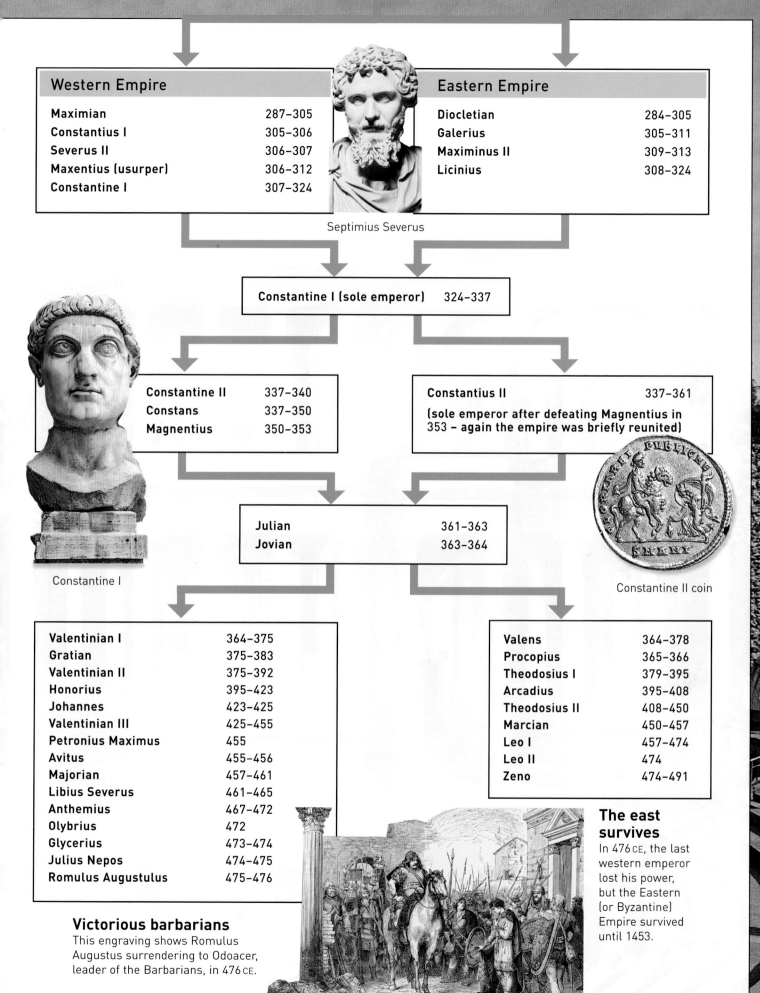

Western Empire

Maximian	287–305
Constantius I	305–306
Severus II	306–307
Maxentius (usurper)	306–312
Constantine I	307–324

Septimius Severus

Eastern Empire

Diocletian	284–305
Galerius	305–311
Maximinus II	309–313
Licinius	308–324

Constantine I (sole emperor)	324–337

Constantine I

Constantine II	337–340
Constans	337–350
Magnentius	350–353

Constantius II	337–361
(sole emperor after defeating Magnentius in 353 – again the empire was briefly reunited)	

Julian	361–363
Jovian	363–364

Constantine II coin

Valentinian I	364–375
Gratian	375–383
Valentinian II	375–392
Honorius	395–423
Johannes	423–425
Valentinian III	425–455
Petronius Maximus	455
Avitus	455–456
Majorian	457–461
Libius Severus	461–465
Anthemius	467–472
Olybrius	472
Glycerius	473–474
Julius Nepos	474–475
Romulus Augustulus	475–476

Valens	364–378
Procopius	365–366
Theodosius I	379–395
Arcadius	395–408
Theodosius II	408–450
Marcian	450–457
Leo I	457–474
Leo II	474
Zeno	474–491

The east survives

In 476 CE, the last western emperor lost his power, but the Eastern (or Byzantine) Empire survived until 1453.

Victorious barbarians

This engraving shows Romulus Augustus surrendering to Odoacer, leader of the Barbarians, in 476 CE.

Find out more

The Roman Empire was extraordinarily rich in archaeological treasures, so most general museums have a Roman collection that is worth visiting. There are also several websites devoted to specific aspects of Roman culture, such as costume or religion. Much of our knowledge of ancient Rome comes from the excavations undertaken at Herculaneum and Pompeii, two towns that were completely devastated by Mount Vesuvius in 79 CE. Layers of volcanic debris have kept buildings and possessions virtually intact, enabling archaeologists to put together an illuminating picture of life in ancient Rome.

Beneath Vesuvius
Visitors can get a glimpse of life in ancient Rome by wandering through the ruined streets and houses of Herculaneum and Pompeii. These plaster casts of a mother and child buried by the volcano (right) are on display at the Museo Archeologico in Naples.

Emperor Hadrian's villa
This country retreat formed part of one of the most splendid estates of the Roman Empire. Many of the buildings were inspired by Hadrian's travels around Egypt and Greece. Open to visitors, the villa is situated near the hilltop town of Tivoli, just outside Rome.

Such ornate urns would have been owned only by the rich

Double-edged sword called a gladius

Ancient artefacts
This spiral-handled urn from the fourth century BCE would have contained oil or wine. It is on display at the Villa Giulia outside Rome, a 16th-century country retreat that now houses the Museo Nationale Etrusco.

Arms and armour
Many museum collections include Roman weapons and armour. Some also display reconstructions, like this short double-edged sword with its own ornate scabbard.

City of Bath

The finest Roman remains in Britain are in the city of Bath, named after its public baths. The Romans called the city *Aquae Sulis* (waters of Sulis, a British goddess) because of its natural hot springs, which reach temperatures of around 37°C (93°F).

Gladius handles were made of wood or bone

Statue of Apollo Belvedere

Vatican Museums

The Vatican Museums are located in several different buildings. The Museo Pio was built especially to display classical statues such as the famous *Apollo Belvedere*.

Shoulder belt, or baldric

USEFUL WEBSITES

- Articles and galleries on all aspects of Roman life:
  www.bbc.co.uk/history/ancient/romans
- Online encyclopedia of Roman emperors:
  www.roman-emperors.org
- Main British Museum website with a link to ancient Rome:
  www.britishmuseum.org
- Main Hermitage Museum website with a link to ancient Rome:
  www.hermitagemuseum.org
- Museum of London's Roman London gallery with a link to ancient Rome:
  www.museumoflondon.org.uk/london-wall/whats-on/galleries/roman-london/

PLACES TO VISIT

POMPEII AND HERCULANEUM

These ruins were first exposed in 1748. Worth seeing are:
- the House of the Faun and the House of the Vettii, villas in western Pompeii
- Pompeii's marketplace.

MUSEO ARCHEOLOGICO NAZIONALE, NAPLES

This historical museum has on display:
- exquisite frescos and mosaics from ruined buildings near Vesuvius
- furnishings and equipment that provide an insight into Roman life.

ROME

Ancient monuments include:
- the Colosseum, now in ruins
- the Forum, with its temples and towers
- Trajan's Forum, containing the 30 m (98 ft) Trajan's column
- The Pantheon, with its splendid dome.

ROMAN BRITAIN

The Romans left behind a number of well-preserved sites, including:
- the Roman baths in the city of Bath
- the Roman Palace and Museum at Fishbourne in West Sussex
- Hadrian's Wall.

ROMAN FRANCE (GAUL)

Southern France is home to:
- the ruins of Roman cities at both Aries and Nîmes, each with an amphitheatre
- the Pont du Gard, a Roman aqueduct.

BRITISH MUSEUM, LONDON, UK

Among the many objects on display are:
- the rare and valuable Portland vase
- the fascinating funeral monument of a Roman couple, Lucius Antistius Sarculo and his wife Antistia.

VATICAN MUSEUMS, ROME, ITALY

The Vatican Museums have an important collection of Roman artefacts, such as:
- a first-century BCE bust of Augustus
- a charming fresco depicting a bride preparing for her wedding.

HERMITAGE MUSEUM, MOSCOW, RUSSIA

Of particular interest are:
- the important sculptural portraits of emperors, statesmen, and ordinary men, women and children
- the remarkable display of bronzes, glassware, ceramics, and mosaics.

Glossary

AMPHITHEATRE Oval-shaped arena, open to the sky.

AMPHORA Two-handled jar with a narrow neck used for transporting and storing wine, olive oil, or other liquids.

Aqueduct

AQUEDUCT An underground or raised channel through which water was brought into Roman towns.

ATRIUM The central hall of a Roman house.

BALDRIC Belt hung from the shoulder, to hold a dagger or a sword.

BALTEUS Belt hung with decorated leather strips that was an important part of the Roman soldier's uniform.

BARBARIAN A term the Romans gave to people living outside the Empire, whom they considered to be uncultured.

BASILICA Public building, usually located in the forum, where legal, business, and ceremonial events took place.

CALIGAE Sturdy military sandals with hobnail soles for reinforcement, designed for frequent long marches.

CATAPULT Military machine used by the Roman army during siege warfare for hurling stones and darts over enemy walls.

CAVALRY Mounted soldiers who were skilled at fighting on horseback.

CENSOR Government official who kept a record of all Roman citizens and revised the membership of the Senate. (*see also* SENATE)

CENTURY Company of 80 men in the Roman army, commanded by a centurion. (*see also* COHORT, LEGION)

CHALCEDONY Type of coloured quartz used for making jewellery.

CHARIOT Wheeled vehicle originally used in war, then in Roman races. Chariots pulled by two horses were called *bigae;* those that were pulled by four horses were called *quadrigae.*

CIRCUS Long stadium where chariot races were held.

CITIZEN Free man (as opposed to a slave), who had privileges such as the right to vote.

CITY-STATE A conventional city that, with its surrounding territory, is also an independent state.

COHORT Sub-division of the Roman army. Each cohort was divided into six centuries. (*see also* LEGION, CENTURY)

CONSUL One of two elected officials who shared the highest position in the Roman Republic.

COUCH Backless seat, on which Romans relaxed and reclined to eat.

DICTATOR A special Roman magistrate appointed with absolute power during state emergencies.

DISTAFF Tool used to hold raw linen or wool fibres.

Catapult

Stone to be thrown went in here

DOMUS Private townhouse, often with a colonnaded back garden.

Chariot race illustrated in mosaic

EMPEROR Absolute ruler of an empire, making "emperor" a higher rank than "king". Augustus Caesar became the first Roman emperor in 27 BCE.

EQUESTRIAN Originally a member of the Roman cavalry, equestrians had to be wealthy enough to buy their own horses. The term later came to mean a rich official whose rank was second only to that of a senator.

FASCES Ceremonial bundle of rods which symbolized legal authority.

FIBULA Brooch used to fasten items of clothing.

FORUM An open area in a Roman town centre, used as a market place and for business.

GALLEY Roman warship powered by one or more rows of oars.

GARUM Strong-tasting sauce made from fish.

A wealthy Roman

GENIUS The personal protective spirit of a man (ancient Roman meaning).

GLADIATOR Trained fighter who battled other gladiators in public contests, sometimes to the death.

GLADIUS Short sword worn by Roman soldiers on their right-hand side.

GOVERNOR Top-ranking official, usually a senator, who administered a Roman province.

HYPOCAUST Central heating system that worked by circulating warm air from a fire under the floor and through cavities in the walls.

INSULA Block of flats made up of multiple rented units.

JUNO The personal protective spirit of a woman.

LAR Spirit who protected a Roman house.

LARARIUM Shrine dedicated to household gods (*lares*), found in every Roman home.

LAUREL Leaves from the bay plant woven into a wreath and worn as a symbol of power.

LEGION Main division of the Roman army containing 3,000–6,000 men (legionaries), organized into ten units called cohorts. (*see also* COHORT)

MORTARIUM Heavy dish made from stone or pottery and used with a hand-held pestle for grinding food.

MOSAIC Floor or wall decoration made from small pieces of glass, stone, or tile.

MUREX Type of mollusc from which precious purple dye was distilled.

ORATOR Skilled public speaker.

PAPYRUS Egyptian water reed whose stem was pressed to make paper-like sheets used for Roman documents.

PATERFAMILIAS Male head of the household, who had absolute power over his wife, children, and servants.

PERISTYLE Colonnaded garden, usually at the back of a Roman house.

PILIUM Heavy, pointed javelin designed to pierce the enemy's shield and armour.

PLAQUE Small slab made of clay, porcelain, or metal and decorated with either an engraving or a raised motif.

PLEBEIAN Roman citizen who was a member of the working class.

PRAETOR High-ranking Roman magistrate, elected annually.

Laurel wreath

PRAETORIAN GUARD Division of elite soldiers founded by Emperor Augustus and responsible for guarding a Roman general or emperor.

PROCURATOR Official responsible for collecting taxes and paying the army and civil service in Roman provinces.

PROVINCE Roman territory that lay outside Italy. Native residents of the provinces were called "provincials".

PUGIO Double-edged dagger worn by Roman soldiers on their left-hand side.

QUAESTOR Elected government official responsible for the finances of the state.

RAISED RELIEF Carved or moulded image that stands out from its background.

REPUBLIC A state where power is held by the people or their representatives, rather than by an emperor or king.

SCABBARD The sheath that holds and protects a sword. A Roman army officer might wear a highly decorated scabbard as a symbol of his position.

Mosaic

SENATE Council of rich noblemen who advised the Roman consuls on matters of law, government, and administration. Members of this council were called senators.

SLAVE Man, woman, or child who is owned by another person as their property, to do work of some kind.

STANDARD Distinctive flag or statuette, especially of a military unit.

THERMOPOLIUM Stall selling hot food on the street in a Roman city or town.

TOGA Formal garment worn by male Roman citizens, which consisted of a length of fabric wrapped around the body and draped over one shoulder. Togas were usually white; those worn by senators had wide purple borders.

TRIBUNE A representative in government, elected by the plebeians to protect their interests, (*see also* PLEBEIAN)

TRIUMPH Procession of honour into Rome by a victorious general and his soldiers, along with their prisoners and plundered treasure.

TUNIC Simple sleeveless shirt, tied at the waist and reaching to the knees, worn by Roman men.

VILLA Luxurious country home belonging to a wealthy Roman family.

Mosaics are made from thousands of tiny pieces of coloured stone

Senator's toga

Index

ABC

Aesculapius, 54, 55
Africa, 7, 25
Alma-Tadema, Sir Lawrence, 39
alphabet (Latin), 40, 64
Alps, 7
amphitheater, 32, 70
amphorae, 60, 70
animals, 22, 28, 32, 60
Anthus, 23
Antistia, 23
Antoninus Pius, 9
Aphrodite, 6
Apollo, 49, 69
aqueducts, 26, 27, 70
architecture, 65
Armitage, Edward A., 46
armor, 10, 11, 13, 14, 33, 50, 68-69
army, 7, 10, 12, 14, 16, 17, 60, 64
art, 6, 64, 66
Artemis, 63
atrium, 24, 27, 70
Attila the Hun, 63
Augustus, 8, 9, 18, 50, 64, 65, 66
Bacchus, 24, 51, 53
baldric, 69, 70
Barbarians, 63, 67, 70
Bath (England), 38, 69
bathing, 27, 38, 39
Ben Hur, 34
bone, 43
Britain, 12, 15, 17, 38, 60, 63
building, 64
Byzantines, 63, 67
Caesar, *see* Julius Caesar
Caledonians, 14
Caligula, 8, 64
Capitoline Hill, 10, 50
Caracalla, 22
Carthage, 7, 60, 64
catapults, 12, 70
cavalry, 13, 70
centurions, 10
chariot racing, 6, 21, 34
Cheshire, 15
children, 20, 22, 56, 58, 64
Christ, 62
Christians, 62, 63
Circus Maximus, 35
citizens, 8, 15, 16, 70
Claudius, 8
coins, 8, 15, 16, 52, 60, 65
Colosseum, 17, 28, 29, 64
Commodus, 30
concrete, 64
Constantine, 62, 67
Constantinople, 62
cooking, 44, 45
cosmetics, 18
crucifixion, 64
Cupid, 24
Cybele, 51, 52

DEF

dance, 48
Diocletian, 62
Dionysus, 51
disease, 54
doctors, 54, 55
dogs, 22
Drusilla, 9
Eastern Empire, 67
education, 18, 20
Egypt, 19, 21, 40, 44
elephants, 7, 25, 32
emperors, 8, 9, 14, 18, 22, 28, 30, 33, 62, 63, 66-67, 70
engineering, 64
England, 12, 14, 15, 38, 43, 53, 63
Etruscans, 6
Europe, 63
fabrics, 13
farming, 58, 59
fasces, 16, 70
Feronia, 22
food, 44, 46, 47, 65
forts, 12
Fortuna, 64
forum, 17, 70
France, 26, 37, 50, 63
funerals, 56, 57
furniture, 24, 25, 65

GHI

gaming, 38
Gaul, 10, 12, 13, 47, 60, 63, 66
Germanicus, 8
Germany, 8, 13
Geta, 22
gladiators, 17, 19, 28, 30, 31, 32, 33, 64
glassware, 42, 46
government, 17, 60
Greece, 6, 36, 64
Hadrian's Villa, 68
Hadrian's Wall, 14, 40
Hannibal, 7, 64
Harness, 13
heating, 65
helmets, 10, 14, 31, 50, 64
herbs, 45, 54
Herculaneum, 64, 68, 69
Hercules, 16, 31, 61, 64
Holland, 13
homes, 23, 24, 25, 65
horses, 13, 34, 35
hunting, 58
Hygeia, 54
ink, 40, 41
Isis, 20, 48, 50, 52
Istanbul, 62
Italy, 6, 7, 36, 49, 58, 60

JKL

javelin, 11, 13
jewelry, 19, 43, 63
Judas, 62
Julia, 9, 18
Julius Caesar, 7, 8, 12, 51, 65
Juno, 9, 50
Jupiter, 50
Kent, 15
lamps, 25
Lancashire, 15
language, 40, 64
Latin, 64
laurel wreaths, 7, 9
legionaries, 10, 11, 12, 13, 14, 15, 64
Livia, 9, 50, 59, 65
Livy, 65
locks, 24
London, 38
Lucius Antistius Sarculo, 23
Lucius Verus, 9

MN

marriage, 22
Mars, 6, 16, 51, 64
Mediterranean, 7, 45
Mercury, 53
metalwork, 42, 43
mime, 36, 37
Minerva, 50
Mithras, 50, 51
mosaics, 24, 36, 37, 48, 58, 65
murex shells, 8
museum collections, 68-69
musical instruments, 48, 49
Naples, 36
Nero, 8
Nile, 59
Nîmes, 69
numerals, 40

OP

Octavian, 8, 66
Odoacer, 67
Orange (France), 37
Oscans, 64
Palmyra, 66
Pan, 48, 51
Pantheon, 65
paterfamilias, 22, 64
Pax Romana, 60
Persians, 62
pilum, 11
Pliny, 54
Pompeii, 24, 25, 41, 42, 45, 47, 57, 59, 68, 69
Pont du Gard, 26
Pope, 63
pottery, 42, 47
Praeneste, 49

RST

Remus, 6
Republic, 6, 8
retiarius, 31, 33
Rhine, 8
roads, 65
Roma, 9
Roman Empire, 7, 12, 14, 40, 50, 60, 62
Roman Peace, 60
Romulus, 6
Rufus, 23
sailing, 60
Samian pots, 42, 47
sandals, 11
Scotland, 14
Senate, 8, 16
senators, 7, 16
slaves, 12, 16, 17, 20, 22, 23, 30, 35, 42, 58, 64
Septimus Severus, 22
Serapis, 50
shield, 11, 12, 30
ships, 7, 60
shops, 65
Snettisham, 43
society, 16
Spain, 7
Spartacus, 64
Stabiae, 25
steelyard, 61
sword, 11, 68

UVW

Uley, 53
Venus, 6, 51
Vercingetorix, 12
Vesuvius, 57, 64, 68
Vesta, 52
Vestal Virgins, 52
Vienne, 50
villas, 58, 59, 68
Vindolanda, 40
Vitruvius, 27
wars, 7, 8, 12, 62
water supply, 26, 27, 65
weapons, 8, 11, 12, 30, 63
weights, 61
Western Empire, 67
wine, 46, 51, 59, 60
women, 18, 19, 21, 34, 36, 37, 38, 43, 50, 52, 64, 65
worship, 23, 50, 51, 52, 53
writing, 40, 41

XYZ

Xanten, 13
York, 14

theater, 36, 37, 48
Thrace, 13
Thracians, 30, 33
Tiber, 55
Tiberius, 8, 9
Titus, 28
toga, 8, 16
toilets, 65
tools, 11, 26, 43
toys, 21
trade, 60, 61
Trajan, 65
Trajan's Column, 40
transport, 60
triumph, 8
tunic, 10, 16, 18
Turkey, 51

Acknowledgments

Dorling Kindersley would like to thank:

The Department of Greek and Roman Antiquities, The British Museum, for providing ancient artifacts for photography; Emma Cox; Celia Clear, British Museum Publications; Mr. B. Cook & Mr. D. Bailey, The Department of Greek and Roman Antiquities; Dr. T.W. Potter & Miss C. Johns, The Department of Prehistoric and Romano-British Antiquities; Mr. D. Kidd & Mr. D. Buckton, The Department of Medieval and Later Antiquities; Peter Connolly for his model of the Colosseum on pp.28-29; Brian Lancaster, Thomas Keenes, Louise Pritchard, Jane Coney, and Lester Cheeseman for their assistance. Ermine Street Guard pp. 10-11; Kathy Lockley for additional picture research; Jane Parker for the index; Julie Ferris for proofreading; Neville Graham, Sue Nicholson, Susan St. Louis for the wallchart, and Hazel Beynon for text editing.

The publisher would like to thank the following for their kind permission to reproduce their photographs:

(Key: a-above; b-below/bottom; c-center; f-far; l-left; r-right; t-top)
Aerofilms 26bc; **Aldus Archive / Syndication International**: 23cl; / Museo Nazionale, Naples 59bl; **Alinari**: / Juseo nazionale, Naples 55bc; **Ancient Art & Architecture Collection**: 38bl, 40c; / R Sheridan 67cr; 68bc; 68cb; **Bridgeman Art Library**: Musee Crozatier, Le Puy en Velay 12cl; / Antiken Museum, Staatliches Museen, W. Berlin 22cr, 25br, 32cl, 39tl, 46bl; **British Film Institute**: 33br; **British Museum**: 12br, 19tl, 19bl, 22tl, 23bl, 42bl, 51tr, 56bl, 57tl, 59c, 64bc, 65bl, 70cla; 71tc; **Capitoline Museums**: 67bc; **J. Allan Cash Photolibrary**: 17cl; **Michael Dixon, Photo Resources**: 19br, 20tl 35bl, 34tr; **Mary Evans Picture Library**: 7br, 8cl, 14tl, 16bl, 18cr, 25c, 30tl, 56tr, 62bc, 63tr; **Werner Forman Archive**: 48bl, 49tr, 53tr, 57br; **Sonia Halliday Photographs**: 32tl, 58cr; **Robert Harding Picture Library**: 37tl, 59tr, 61tr; / Tony Waltham 68tl; **Simon James**: 12br, 14cr, 24cl, 26tl 27cl, 27cr, 28bl, 35tl 37tc, 38tl 44c, 45tr, 50cr, 57; **Kobal Collection**: 34cl; **Louvre / © Reunion des Musees Nationaux**: 20-21b; **Mansell Collection**: 7t, 13tl; **Rex Features**: 33br; **Jaap Bitendijk** 33crb; **Scala**: 25bl; / Citta del Vaticano, Rome 13tr, 48cl; /Museo della Terme, Rome 18bl; / Musei Capitolini, Rome 36tl; / Museo Nazionale, Naples 36br, 41tl / Museo Civico, Albenga 60cl; **The Vatican**: 69c

Wallchart: **DK Images**: British Museum cl, tr; Ermine Street Guard c, cb, clb (pilum), clb (sword and dagger), tc; National Maritime Museum cra (ship); Rough Guides tl; **Getty Images**: Bridgeman Art Library fbr

Jacket: *Front*: Dorling Kindersley: The British Museum tc, tr, tr (brooches), ftr; Ermine Street Guard cb, c. *Back*: Dorling Kindersley: The British Museum tr, cl, fbr, crb; Peter Connolly - modelmaker bl, Ermine Street Guard tl.

Illustrations: Peter Bull, 27; 38; Eugene Fleury 7

All other images © Dorling Kindersley

For further information see: www.dkimages.com